$9.95

THE CHARACTER AND INFLUENCE OF THE
INDIAN TRADE IN WISCONSIN

FREDERICK JACKSON TURNER

THE CHARACTER
AND INFLUENCE
OF THE INDIAN TRADE
IN WISCONSIN

*A Study of the Trading Post
as an Institution*

*Edited and
with an Introduction by*
DAVID HARRY MILLER
and WILLIAM W. SAVAGE, JR.

UNIVERSITY OF OKLAHOMA PRESS
NORMAN

"The Character and Influence of the Indian Trade in Wisconsin" was originally published in Herbert Baxter Adams (ed.), *Johns Hopkins University Studies in Historical and Political Science*, Ninth Series, Vol. XI–XII (November and December, 1891) , pp. 547–615.

Library of Congress Cataloging in Publication Data

Turner, Frederick Jackson, 1861–1932.
The character and influence of the Indian trade in Wisconsin.

Originally presented as the author's thesis, Johns Hopkins University.
Reprint of the 1891 ed. which was originally issued as no. 11–12 of Education, history and politics, which forms the 9th series of Johns Hopkins University studies in historical and political science.
Includes bibliographical references.
1. Indians of North America—Wisconsin—Trading posts. 2. Indians of North America—Trading posts. 3. Fur trade—United States. 4. Wisconsin—History—To 1848. I. Series. II. Series: Johns Hopkins University. Studies in historical and political science; 9th ser., no. 11–12. III. Series: Education, history, and politics; no. 11–12.
H31.E25 no. 11–12, 1976 [E78.W8] 300'.8s [381] 76–47331

CONTENTS

EDITORS' INTRODUCTION

There can be no doubt, whatever one sees as the value of his work or its validity, that Frederick Jackson Turner was a figure of central importance in the development of a professionalized historiography in the United States. The testimony in this regard is overwhelming, and, since his death, Turner has consistently been pointed out by professional historians themselves as one of the very few major figures. One might even say that a consensus of the professions exists on that point. On an occasion when the American Historical Association requested the executive council to prepare a list of the most important American historians, Turner was the only professionally trained historian to receive first rank.[1] That, however, is almost the only point on which general agreement can be secured, and as one surveys the voluminous literature concerning Turner, the over-all impression

---

[1] Ray Allen Billington, *Frederick Jackson Turner: Historian, Scholar, Teacher* (New York: Oxford University Press, 1973), pp. 420–21.

one receives is that his significance has largely, though certainly not entirely, been misunderstood.

Leaving the debate over frontier or sectional historiography aside, for the moment, one must make the fundamental point that Turner's seminal 1893 essay, "The Significance of the Frontier in American History," is probably of least importance for what it says about the frontier. As fundamental—and obstructive—as Turner's essay has been in the development of American frontier historiography, that cannot entirely explain its importance. It is the theoretical form, not the specific content, of the frontier essay which is of chief importance. With the frontier essay, Turner articulated what would become the controlling paradigm[2] of American historiography through at least the first half of the twentieth century.

The theoretical context in which Turner's work must be understood, then, is that of the breakdown of the consensus within the profession regarding the dominant research model of the time, the pseudo-Rankean, or "scientific," historiography characteristic of the newly emergent historical seminars in eastern universities of the late nineteenth century. Despite the "splendid confidence"[3] of the proponents of the pseudo-Rankean school in the 1880's and 1890's, the flaws of their approach were many, serious, and, superficially at least, obvious to many contemporaries in the intellectual disciplines. Indeed, the scientific character of the pesudo-Rankean historiography was largely miscon-

2 For a general discussion of the nature and role of paradigms in the development of science, consult Thomas S. Kuhn, *The Structure of Scientific Revolutions* (2d ed., Chicago: University of Chicago Press, 1970).

3 The phrase is John Higham's. John Higham, Leonard Krieger, and Felix Gilbert, *History: The Development of Historical Studies in the United States* (Englewood Cliffs, N.J.: Prentice-Hall, Inc., 1965), p. 90.

ceived, and the attitude most intended to be carried by the term was no more than a reaction against a romanticized perception of history. Both in interpretive form and in content, "scientific" historiography viewed the individual in society as subordinate to institutions, which could be objectively treated as concrete phenomena. The pseudo-Rankeans did, to be sure, emphasize a critical approach to evidence, primarily in documentary forms, but so far as the *analysis* of the phenomena was concerned (which must ultimately be understood as the whole point of scientific study), their attitude was almost entirely negative. Basically, the pseudo-Rankeans failed to understand the distinction between speculative generalizations of a metahistorical character and the working hypotheses of active investigation. Their understanding of inductive methodology in science excluded the formulation of either working hypotheses or generalized judgments.[4] Yet, ironically enough, not only did they not understand the way in which their work inescapably involved unarticulated generalizations, but also their articulated idealization of the theory of social progress involved them, whether they knew it or not, in adherence to what they abhorred most, a speculative philosophy of history.[5]

Between 1910 and 1930 a strong current of dissent manifested itself, and two fundamental criticisms were raised. First, it was pointed out that the dry realism of the pseudo-Rankean approach to history had resulted in its becoming virtually unreadable, so that history no longer appealed to a

[4] John Hermann Randall, Jr., and George Haines IV, "Controlling Assumptions in the Practice of American Historians," *Theory and Practice in Historical Study* (Social Sciences Research Council Bulletin 54; New York, 1945), p. 32.

[5] Higham, *et. al., History*, pp. 92–101.

ix

broad public. Historians were simply becoming isolated from the general reading public as they became professionals. Second, a number of practitioners in other social sciences were in the process of pointing out that history, since it was not nomothetic, was not scientific either. Associated with the critiques of other social sciences was the drawback that some of these more rapidly expanding disciplines were involved increasingly with studies oriented toward contemporary issues and problems and so were commanding more general attention. The eventual product of this situation was that, while older, more conservative historians backed themselves further into intellectual isolation, a younger generation, moved by the "progressive" spirit of the times, announced, in the period between 1910 and 1912, the advent of a New History.[6]

The central tenets of the credo of the New Historiography were seemingly straightforward responses to perceived flaws in the Old Historiography. Ostensibly, the positive recommendations of the New Historiography centered around two goals: to use history to account for the present condition; and to approach historical problems from a wider perspective than the merely political, focusing attention, not on the purely formal, constitutional structure of institutions, but rather on the various "forces" responsible for both the form and the moving spirit of institutions. The presentism of the New Historiography carried with it not only a recognition of the subjective aspects of historical study, but also an embracing of subjectivism as the desired norm, and, ultimately, the assertion of the basic relativity of historical knowledge. At the same time, the New Historians recognized the need for significant generalizations,

6 *Ibid.*, pp. 104–10.

which, since they were not to be historically divined, must be acquired by assiduous study of the sister sciences of society.[7]

Interestingly enough, Turner appears to have anticipated all of the major ideas of the New Historians. In 1891 and 1892, Turner wrote two essays of a semitheoretical nature: "The Significance of History" (published in the *Wisconsin Journal of Education*, Volume 21 [1891], 230–34) and "Problems of American History" (published in *Aegis*, Volume 7 [1892], 48–52). In these essays all of the ideas of the New History were foreshadowed. The role of the historian, said Turner, was to account for present conditions, for the present may understand itself only by understanding its past.[8] This implied, for Turner, that the historian must rewrite his history in reference to the present condition, *and his own background*.[9] Moreover, the purpose of historical writing was frankly utilitarian (to aid in training good citizens),[10] and this implied that the historian must expose, not the common features of the institutions of various nations, but the uniqueness of American institutions as imposed by the peculiar forces working within American society itself.[11]

From a modern vantage point, it seems obvious that Turner was a New Historian, and surely Ray Allen Billington was correct when he said that, had "The Significance of

[7] Harry Elmer Barnes, *A History of Historical Writing* (2d ed., New York: Dover Publications, 1962), pp. 379–86. Barnes was a major publicist of the general outlook of the New Historiography.

[8] "Problems in American History," in Fulmer Mood (ed.), *Early Writings of Frederick Jackson Turner* (Madison: University of Wisconsin Press, 1938), p. 72.

[9] "The Significance of History," in Mood (ed.), *Early Writings*, pp. 52, 55.

[10] *Ibid.*, p. 58.

[11] "Problems in Amercan History," p. 73.

History" been written by an eastern-establishment historian and published in a review of national reputation, it would have been the generally recognized charter of the New History.[12] The whole point, however, is that Frederick Jackson Turner was not merely in anticipation of the movement but, in some sense, its founder. To understand this, it must be understood that the New History as a viable movement in American historiography was not the product of theoretical treatises. None of the speculative pieces ordinarily identified as fundamental to the movement, from James Harvey Robinson's *The New History* to Carl Becker's "Everyman his Own Historian," were anything but afterthought—attempts to explain practices already in use. Neither were Turner's two early historiographical essays the source of the New History. Rather, the opening shot of the New History's assault on the bastion of the historical establishment was "The Significance of the Frontier in American History." The significance of the "Significance" is that it provided the prototype of an interpretive model for history which was widely circulated in the twenty years after its first presentation. It advanced the ideas of the New History not in abstraction, not in general terms, but in the suggestion of *specific* approaches to *specific* problems—approaches which *implied* the more general ideas characteristic of the New History.[13]

Many historians in the 1890's were uneasy about some of the implications of the pseudo-Rankean approach, but what

12 Ray Allen Billington, *The Genesis of the Frontier Thesis* (San Marino, Calif.: The Huntington Library, 1971), pp. 47–48.

13 Compare Joseph Schafer, "Turner's Frontier Philosophy," in O. Lawrence Burnette, Jr., (comp.), *Wisconsin Witness to Frederick Jackson Turner: A Collection of Essays on the Historian and the Thesis* (Madison: The State Historical Society of Wisconsin, 1961), p. 28, and Lee Benson, *Toward the Scientific Study of History* (Philadelphia: J. B. Lippincott, 1972), p. 189.

produced real historiographical change was Turner's perception that the "germ" theory of institutions, as taught by his major professor at the Johns Hopkins University, Herbert Baxter Adams, could not explain the American West. Turner's reaction against the reigning paradigm was almost entirely tied to the objection that eastern historians ignored the West and that the West was important, not because it was a region close to Turner's heart, but because it presented an anomaly unanticipated by the dominant theory.

> It was that there was a persistent pervasive influence in American life, which did not get its full attention from those who thought in terms of North and South, as well as from those who approached the West as fighting ground, or as ground for exploration history.[14]

But Turner's objections on this subject were far more concerned with method—total outlook—than with mere content, or lack of content, so far as the West was concerned. Many writers have expended much energy dealing with the influences of Turner's frontier background and environment in the attempt to explain the origins of his frontier interpretation, but the most critical influence on Turner was, quite simply, that he was a young American historian in the 1890's.

Hence, it was Turner's search for an explanation of the role of the American West which culminated in the statement that "the existence of an area of free land, its continuous recession, and the advancement of American settlement westward explain American development" that explains the

[14] Frederick Jackson Turner to Constance Lindsay Skinner, March 15, 1922, in Wilbur R. Jacobs, *The Historical World of Frederick Jackson Turner* (New Haven: Yale University Press, 1968), p. 61.

development of the New History.[15] From the practical suggestions made in his 1893 essay and, later, from his teaching of graduate students and his own further publication on western state-making, sections, and so on, the interpretive ideas fundamental to the presentist-relativist school developed and were propagated. The emphasis placed on the uniqueness of American development, the obvious assertion that America was *not* to be explained as a bundle of European institutions merely transplanted to new soil, implied more than a challenge to the old historiography.[16] Indeed, it involved the denial that history—in the sense of the European past—had any real effect on *our* American present. The American wilderness de-Europeanized the European.[17] It made something new out of him. And the result was a unique people, strong, independent in both mind and spirit, practical, difficult to control, and democratic in attitude.[18] If the crucible of the frontier liberated the immigrant, what it liberated him from was the European past.[19] The role of history was to develop the "self consciousness" of the present, and the role of the frontier was to lend itself to that purpose.[20] But the frontier could only be so used if it were assumed that historical truth was relative to the present and its purpose. For Turner, then, the historian could not know the past as it really was. Rather, he had to

[15] "The Significance of the Frontier in American History," in Mood (ed.), *Early Writings*, p. 186.

[16] *Ibid.*, pp. 187–88.

[17] "Western State-Making in the Revolutionary Era," *American Historical Review*, Vol. I (1895), pp. 70–72.

[18] "Significance of the Frontier in American History," pp. 188, 211, 220. Compare with "Colonization of the West," *American Historical Review*, Vol. XI (1906), pp. 303–304.

[19] "Significance of the Frontier in American History," p. 211.

[20] "Problems in American History," p. 72.

seek its "significance," and its significance, if it was to be relevant, had to be determined by the present.[21]

By the time the New Historians advanced their theoretical arguments in 1912 and later, Turner's ideas had been working their effect on American historical thinking for almost twenty years. The New Historians were doing no more than giving general form to ideas implicit in Turner's practice and ideas that they had learned, whether directly or indirectly, from him. The significance of the "Significance," then, had little to do with the frontier. Rather it is this very point—that Frederick Jackson Turner's practical suggestions implied general ideas (ones he had already advanced) which could be applied to specific problems other than the frontier—which explains how a scholar concerned with a limited field, one that never commanded a majority interest in the American historical profession, could be generally recognized as one of the two or three most important figures in the whole of the history of American historiography. The special theory of the frontier carried, then, a general theory of history.

The obvious question at this point, of course, concerns the relation of all this to Turner's dissertation, here reprinted. Given the understanding that the frontier essay was a vehicle for the statement of an alternative approach to historical study, if not altogether a repudiation of the pseudo-Rankeans, how did the dissertation relate to either the old or the new research models? Certainly it is our feeling that it occupies an important position in the development of Turner's approach, although it is perhaps more

---

[21] "Social Forces in American History," *American Historical Review*, Vol. XVI (1911), p. 231, and Frederick Jackson Turner to Merle Curti, August 27, 1928, in Billington, *Genesis of the Frontier Thesis*, p. 279.

important as an indication of other possibilities than the one he indeed finally chose. The point is that the dissertation carries in it only a most tentative suggestion of Turner's later frontier idea, and were it not for the fame of that formulation of 1893, this earlier trace would go largely unnoticed. The dissertation is, however, of much greater interest, in that Turner used it to make a number of more sober generalizations, which, had they been exploited in the tone in which they were advanced, would make it possible to see Turner as indeed the founder of a realistic comparative approach.

The dissertation begins with a discussion of the trading post, seen roughly as a "germ" institution.[22] This survey is brief and somewhat superficial, and, for these reasons, greatly misleading. It has been maintained, in a view probably representative of most historians' attitudes toward the dissertation, that this "comparative" side of the piece was only a respectful but meaningless concession to Turner's mentor at the Hopkins, Herbert Baxter Adams.[23] Its real significance, however, was far greater. We must keep in mind that, even in his adoption of a more radical alternative approach than the one taught by Adams, Turner did not fundamentally reject the "germ" theory. His objection was that the proponents of the "germ" theory applied it too literally to American experience and so failed to understand the American experience.[24] And that, after all, was an observation he made *after* the dissertation. So far as the "germ" theory and the dissertation are concerned, it is vital to note

[22] See below, pp. 3–6.
[23] Jacobs, *The Historical World of Frederick Jackson Turner*, p. 11, and Billington, *Frederick Jackson Turner*, p. 72.
[24] "Problems in American History," p. 74.

his statement that, whereas in the Mediterranean basin the effect of the trading post and trade between a more and a less advanced people was beneficent, in the context of white-Indian contact in North America it had proved destructive to Indian society.[25] Having made this revealing observation, he then went on to examine the role of trade between whites and Indians as illuminating the general question of such trade between primitive and sophisticated cultures.[26]

This involved, of course, some critique of the "germ" altogether for a far more sophisticated comparative approach, in which attention was shifted from the near-genetic continuity of institutional structures implied in the "germ" theory to the analysis of functional relationships between cultures wherein the trading post served as the focal point for economic, social, and political interaction. The result of all this, in terms of the content of the dissertation itself, is most interesting, for it led Turner to the formulation, however inexplicit, of a series of highly cogent hypotheses of obvious importance not only because of their comparative application but also because they so obviously contrast, in logical terms, with the frontier ideas for which he is so highly reputed.

In the course of his work, then, Turner developed two

[25] See below, p. 6.

[26] This was an idea that had apparently occupied him for some time. Frederick Jackson Turner to William F. Allen, December 31, 1888, in Jacobs, *Historical World of Frederick Jackson Turner*, p. 132: ". . . I am becoming more than ever impressed with the fact that the French exploration, occupation and struggle for the Northwest, and the secrets of its hold over that region, were not religious, nor chiefly personal, but that primarily they were governed by economic considerations—and I believe that the economic relations of civilized with primitive man is a neglected chapter of history in general . . . ."

series of hypotheses. The first was concerned with the question of the effect on Indian society of white intrusion into the frontier environment and permits application to the wider question of the effect of the intrusion of any "advanced" society in the environment of "primitive" peoples. The second series of observations was concerned with one aspect of this contact and its effect on the development of white society as manifested in large-scale political and economic developments. Taken as a group, the ideas advanced by Turner on these subjects constitute not only a series of significant hypotheses offered in explanation of some major aspects of white-Indian contact, but also a series of potential working hypotheses that might be tested in other contexts. They are important enough, especially in contrast with the content of the frontier essay of 1893, for some of the more general to be mentioned explicitly. What follows then, is only the roughest sort of paraphrase.

The intrusion of an advanced society into the environment of a primitive society of hunters, through commercial contacts, may involve the disruption of the normal patterns of social behaviour within the primitive society

by causing the focus of economic life to be changed from hunting for subsistence to hunting to acquire goods for trade, thus changing not only the routine of normal life but also the relation to the environment;

by introducing, as trade goods, products of the technology of the advanced society which may tend to alter the level of military technology for one or more local units of the primitive society, thus destroying any prior pattern of power relations; and/or

by introducing, as trade goods, products of the technology of the advanced society which may raise the level of economic expectation within the primitive society beyond the productive capacity of its own technology, hence reducing the primitive society to dependence upon the traders.[27]

This is by no means a complete list of the ideas Turner developed in the dissertation, but it is sufficient to give an impression of the flavor of the dissertation for purposes of comparison to the frontier essay.

We also find tucked away in the dissertation, however, the bones of another idea subsequently developed by Turner in the 1893 essay, concerning the *progression* of stages of social complexity on the frontier, complete with the implied *necessity* of that progression, as one type of frontier follows another in any given region, leading ultimately to Civilization.[28] This, of course, is merely the precursor of his later flight of rhetorical fancy in the frontier essay:

> Stand at Cumberland Gap and watch the procession of civilization, marching single file—the buffalo, following the trail to the salt springs, the Indian, the fur-trader and hunter, the cattle raiser, the pioneer farmers—and the frontier has passed by. Stand at South Pass in the Rockies a century later and see the same procession with wider intervals between.[29]

The comparison between these two works is not idly made, and it reveals stark contrast. The hypotheses of the dissertation, compared with those of the frontier essay, offered genuine possibilities, not only for comparative research, but also *as a remedy to the criticisms current in the late nineteenth century that history was by its very nature incapable of developing generalized analytic statements susceptible of being tested on their validity or non-validity*

[27] See below, pp. 32–33, 36–37, 40, 69–71, 74–75, 77–78.
[28] See below, pp. 18, 79–85 and compare with "Significance of the Frontier in American History," pp. 187, 196.
[29] "Significance of the Frontier in American History," p. 199.

in a general sense. Doubtless the hypotheses of the dissertation could have been formulated in more abstract form. They might also have been reduced to yet more abstract and general theoretical statements. But that is not really the point. The point is that the dissertation did have, in a time when history was not supposed to be nomothetic, a nomothetic aspect which could, and still can, be defended as theoretically sound. These hypotheses, after being tested, might be rejected; but that they could be tested at all, that they could be treated, even with some reformulation, perhaps, as legitimate propositions at all, is of considerable importance. The frontier essay, by contrast, does not have the same virtue. Indeed, and despite years of discussion by American historians of the frontier hypothesis supposedly advanced in the essay of 1893, that very famous piece contains no hypothesis. There are a few vague notions which with considerable effort and tinkering, might be reduced to some more formal structure. But that would be the same as introducing a different set of ideas.

What *is* the frontier hypothesis? Is it the theory that the availability of free land determined the development of various aspects of American character? Or is it the notion that on the frontier society relives each successive stage in the universal process of social evolution? Is it both? In 1941 a questionnaire asking historians to comment on the Turner hypothesis revealed that significant numbers of scholars felt that it ought not to be investigated at all or that it should not be too explicitly defined.[30] If it were defined it would prove to be precisely the sort of "grand

[30] George W. Pierson, "American Historians and the Frontier Hypothesis in 1941," in Burnette, *Wisconsin Witness to Frederick Jackson Turner*, pp. 122, 125–26.

design" theory of history, deterministic and ultimately un-verifiable, that historians in general always have professed to abhor.[31] In short, the vague notions of the frontier essay of 1893 are obviously absurd from either a logical or a purely historical point of view, while the dissertation presents easily articulated, usable, verifiable hypotheses obviously drawn from evidence. Yet, while the dissertation is known mostly to the specialists interested in its specific subject matter, the eassay was swallowed whole by the profession, to become, as has been observed, "holy writ"[32] or an incan-tation,[33] presumably to conjure with.

A clear understanding of the theoretical context of Turner's frontier interpretation and of the New History that developed therefrom demands, once again, reference to the theoretical problems of the pseudo-Rankean, or "sci-entific," historiography. The reason for this is that they shared common views on some major questions and that the flaws in the theoretical aspects of the New Historiography stem from these common assumptions.

The major flaw in American "scientific" historiography as it was developing in the late nineteenth century was its fundamental antagonism to historical theory, or, more pre-cisely, to the consideration of theoretical questions as a serious activity for historians.[34] There were, of course, some fairly obvious specific reasons for this. For one thing, the somewhat prosaic realism of scientific historiography, a

[31] This, despite various disclaimers to the contrary, as in Avery Craven, "Frederick Jackson Turner, Historian," in *ibid.*, p. 108.

[32] Billington, *Frederick Jackson Turner*, pp. 447–48.

[33] Richard Hofstadter, "Turner and the Frontier Myth," *American Scholar*, 18 (1949), p. 435.

[34] W. Stull Holt, "The Idea of Scientific History in America," *Journal of the History of Ideas*, Vol. 1 (1940), p. 354. See also Higham, *et. al., History*, p. 99.

product of the general antiromantic attitude of the profession, carried with it a general distrust of fanciful speculations such as those that had formerly gone under the name "philosophies of history."[35] Second, philosophy itself, as understood by American scholars in the late nineteenth century, consisted mainly of a sort of moralizing most appropriately identified, albeit in a vague sense, with philosophy of religion.[36] In short, considering the way in which American historians understood philosophy, it is not difficult to imagine why they wanted no part of it. The basic problem, however, was that antagonism to theorizing or philosophizing involved considerable philosophical naïveté. Consequently, historians knew so little about theory that they were unable to avoid even the most elemental errors. This was reflected in their almost total misapprehension of the ideas of the putative patron saint of American scientific historiography, Leopold van Ranke,[37] and, of vastly greater importance, in their almost primitive understanding of the whole idea of science and scientific method.

It is the way in which these men understood science, then, that is central to the contemporary objections to "scientific" historiography in the late nineteenth century. They did not know what science was, and their philosophical background would not enhance their understanding of method.

As a result of these factors, historians experienced a basic confusion of method with technique. It is quite clear that the scientific historians failed to understand that scientific method has to do with the way in which one *thinks* about data. Indeed, they seem to have had a mechanical view of

[35] Higham, *et al.*, *History*, p. 98.
[36] *Ibid.*
[37] Bert J. Lowenberg, *American History in American Thought* (New York: Simon & Schuster, 1972), p. 385.

xxii

method. It caused them to look on experimental technique, for example, as a methodological problem (as, in general, they viewed any process of gathering data), as opposed to intellectually processing it, which should have been *the* methodological issue.[38] For this reason, they made the understandable assumption that if they religiously observed the guidelines for critical handling of source materials they would be scientific in method. For this reason, too, their view of scientific methodology in history was almost entirely restricted to the question of data collection.[39] The issue of what one does with data was almost never raised.

The same basic problem manifested itself in another respect as well: the understanding of inductive reasoning. It was quite obvious that, to the scientific historian, induction involved only the collection of data and that categorization and the development of conceptually generalized types had no role. Hence, they were totally opposed to the formation of generalized judgments as an end result, or goal, of historical inquiry and were equally opposed to the use of critical working hypotheses. Their understanding of induction led them to the assumption that the facts would speak for themselves,[40] which, by implication, committed them to a difficult epistemological position. If the New Historians went overboard in adopting epistemological skepticism, the "scientific" historians went overboard in the other direction, adopting—only by implication, of course—a radically realist epistemology. This led them to two further assump-

[38] Randall and Haines, "Controlling Assumptions in the Practice of American Historians," p. 32.

[39] A view restated by Louis Gottschalk, *Understanding History* (New York: Random House, 1950), p. 8: "History is, to be sure, scientific in method; millions of historical facts can be established as convincingly, for layman and expert alike, as that two and two make four . . . ."

[40] Holt, "The Idea of Scientific History in America," p. 359.

tions, both dependent on the assumption that any generalized statement about phenomena must represent the *real*
condition of the phenomena, or *real* relationships, which
had only to be described—which is another way of saying
that the facts will speak for themselves. Obviously, this being
the case, the scientist must be a sort of *tabula rasa*, contribut-
ing nothing in terms of analysis but only uncovering the
phenomena. All of this was consistent with their understanding that the methodological problem consisted of
nothing other than the collection of data. But it also involved the assumption of a *real* distinction, both epistemo-
logically and ontologically, between natural and social
phenomena. The natural scientist could make generalized
statements because of an intrinsic characteristic of natural
phenomena which permitted, or even led him, to do so,
while the most essential characteristic of social phenomena
was, of course, that they were by nature unique and not
susceptible of generalization.[41] In other words, there could
be laws of natural science because such laws were a part of
nature itself and became obvious when the facts of nature
were properly known. Hence follows the meaning of "law"
in scientific terms, as assumed by the scientific historians;
namely, they saw "law" in science (and nature) as being
analogous to some sort of legislative enactment, rather than
as a tentative statement concerning regularities as perceived
by the human mind.[42] And, of course, it went without saying

[41] On this issue, see Fred Morrow Fling, "Historical Synthesis," *American
Historical Review*, Vol. 9 (1903), pp. 1–22. Fling presents a discussion of all
these matters as a part of an extended review of the work of several European
writers on the logic of historical inquiry. Fling himself was philosophically
sophisticated enough to understand many of the fallacies mentioned in this
section, but his article indicates the kind of assumptions current at the
time he wrote.

[42] A good example of the way in which the term "law" was understood

that any variety of general proposition—hypothesis, theory, or whatever—was law in this sense.

The result of these various assumptions was a general insistence in the profession on a totally antinomian posture, emphasizing the study of social phenomena only as unique and discrete particulars. It seems not to have occurred to these gentlemen that if the social world consisted completely of irregularities it would be unknowable or that, in any case, irregularities have meaning only by comparison with regularities.

Hence the ground for the dissatisfaction with the "scientific" school of historiography seems clear, even if those who found it wanting failed to analyze the situation clearly. The result was a sort of quiet intellectual crisis. Historians became somewhat defensive when they acknowledged criticism, and the older, more established elements in the profession, who had perhaps more of a stake in the existing notions of historiography, generally retreated into intellectual isolationism. The only major attempt to cope with criticism involved conceding some points to the critics, granting that perhaps social phenomena could be the subject of generalization; but if that were so, historians argued, the task should be left to sociologists.[43] The attempt, then, was to save traditional historiography by defining history as a "particularizing science," a contradiction in terms. No cogent reason was ever supplied for this totally unwarranted distinction between what sociologists properly did and what historians properly did, and apparently historians committed themselves to the doctrine that history was all it could

may be found in Edward F. Cheyney, "Law in History," *American Historical Review*, Vol. 29 (1924), pp. 231–48.

[43] A position adopted, curiously enough, by Fling, "Historical Synthesis."

be. In short, the reaction, psychologically understandable but intellectually unsound, was that, since historians in the past had always dealt with individual phenomena in an intellecually unsystematic manner, they must continue to do the same in the future.

The problem for younger, less established men was equally severe. They had been led to see their discipline as a science, participating in the great intellectual enterprise on an equal basis, only to be told by those more securely entrenched in the scientific community itself that it was not. The lack of nomothetic judgments, in combination with the fact that historians studied the past, led to a discouraging conclusion that history must be irrelevant, a notion made no more palatable by the increasing involvement of other social sciences in the pressing issues of contemporary social problems. But unfortunately the younger men like Turner were not any better trained, either philosophically or scientifically. As a result, the New Historiography was based on some of the same general preconceptions of what science was. It was based on the old assumptions that natural phenomena were not essentially unique, while social phenomena were; that scientific laws were objective elements of nature itself, rather than subjective human concepts to explain phenomena as they appeared to man; that, in other words, the phenomena imposed method on the enquirer.[44] Sharing these assumptions, but not wishing to back themselves into an isolated corner, the New Historians could not salvage

[44] There is some indication that historians were beginning to revise their conception of science in general. See W. M. Sloan. "The Substance and Vision of History," *American Historical Review*, Vol. 17 (1912), pp. 243–44. Compare with Frederick Jackson Turner to Carl Becker, February 13, 1926, in Billington, *Genesis of the Frontier Thesis*, p. 247: "No there's no science of history. Sometimes I doubt that there is a real science (in the sense that cuts out history) of anything."

history as science, and, their use of terminology aside, they stopped trying.

The result was the presentist-relativist-subjectivist orientation of the New Historiography. If history had lost by not being scientific, it gained accordingly by being freed from restraint. If historical phenomena could not be the subject of historical generalizations, historians could leave that to sociologists or economists and then borrow from those scholars' stocks of theoretical concepts.[45] And they could compensate for the implied irrelevance of antinomian history by dealing with the present.[46] But, somehow, presentism carried subjectivism in its train. If the historian used the past to explain the present, he must surely be interpreting the past in the light of the present—more particularly *his* present.[47] Hence, without admitting it in so many words, the New History went from the doctrine that the facts spoke for themselves to the implicit assumption that the facts were meaningless and could be made to say anything. By this means, the New Historiography opened the back door to generalization after the front had been definitively closed. One could not make laws, but one could "interpret," and by merely interpreting and not claiming to be nomothetic, one evaded the charge of misusing the facts.

Quite naturally, relativism and skepticism were also involved in the New Historiography's analysis of the nature

45 Higham, *et al.*, *History*, p. 114.

46 Carl Becker, "Some Aspects of the Influence of Social Problems and Ideas upon the Study and Writing of History," *Publications of the American Sociological Society*, Vol. 7 (1913), p. 93.

47 *Ibid.*, p. 73. Compare with Carl Becker to Frederick Jackson Turner, May 16, 1910, in Jacobs, *Historical World of Frederick Jackson Turner*, p. 207: "We must have a past that is the product of all the present. That, I take it, is the same as saying that history is the self-consciousness of humanity."

xxvii

of the historical enterprise, but with an equally appalling lack of sophistication. For instance, the subjective present-ism of the New History was tied up with the idea that the influence exerted on one's judgment and interpretations demanded that, in reviewing a given historian's interpreta-tions, one must first deal with his background. The question was asked, why did he say such and so? Because he was a Protestant? Because he was raised in Portage, Wisconsin, when it was still a frontier town? The question should have been whether or not the interpretation was accurate. But this demanded some sort of common and intelligible canon of judgment, a canon which did not exist. Its development would require serious and sophisticated intellectual effort. But, in a sense, that was unimportant since the New History was committed to the implicit proposition that the validity of an interpretation was of distinctly secondary importance (really, there could be no objectively valid interpretation) alongside the question of the purpose it served. The con-clusion must be that any interpretation was admissible so long as it was acceptable in respect to its purpose and was advanced by a professional.

The results of all this can be seen clearly in the work of Frederick Jackson Turner. It can be seen in his use, without much investigation, of general concepts, untested so far as he could know, drawn from other sciences. It can be seen in the advancing of reckless generalizations expressed in a logically chaotic form. It can be seen in that these general-izations were cast in a "grand design" form clearly intended to answer the demand for meaningful history at a time when history seemed meaningless, at least in American terms. It can be seen in the subordination of history to essentially nonhistorical purposes, so that bias, rather than an appeal

to evidence or logic, was ultimately the criterion of accept-
ability.[48] And as Turner led, so a younger generation followed.[49] That neither Turner nor his professional adherents
saw that the very form of the New History involved them in
crucial misconceptions and contradictions—that it involved
the denial of the very possibility of historical knowledge—
is due basically to the revulsion of the American historical
profession for the consideration, and teaching, of historical
theory. It is due, that is, to the fundamental anti-intellectual-
ism that has dominated the American historical profession.

Nothing could be so glaringly out of place in this context
than Turner's dissertation. The answer to the question of
why it did not become a model for further research is
patently obvious. The progressive spirit of the age of the
New History did not want history, properly conceived. No
one has succeeded in putting it better than John Higham,
who observed that the New Historians were the philosophes
of an unhistorical age.[50] But the mere existence of the
Turner dissertation raises the haunting possibility that
something better was possible had the temper of the profession been prepared for it.

Finally, if Turner's dissertation suggests implications for
the study of American historiography as a whole, it also
invites specific comment upon that particular field within

[48] An interesting aspect of Turner's life to consider in this context is his
activity in connection with the National Board for Historical Service in
World War I. Frederick Jackson Turner to Max Farrand, May 5, 1917, in
Jacobs, *Historical World of Frederick Jackson Turner*, p. 146: "They will
feel a sense of treason to the cause if they are all silent while pacifists set
forth the meaning of American history . . . ."

[49] Randall and Haines, "Controlling Assumptions in the Practice of
American Historians," pp. 43–50, show an appreciation of Turner's role in
the advent of the New History.

[50] Higham, *et. al., History*, p. 112.

the discipline to which Turner's 1893 essay gave rise—
Western American history. Scholars in the field have be-
moaned the fact that it has lately attracted the most pedes-
trian of minds and that it is almost totally devoid of any
sort of methodology. Confronted by the gradual but steady
deterioration of the field in recent years—deterioration
marked by its diminishing power to attract good students
and the frequently trivial nature of its literature—some
observers have warned of its impending demise. But other
diagnoses are more encouraging: fresh interpretations of
familiar themes, some practitioners suggest, may yet allow
Western history to survive. Still others, building on Turner's essay or paraphrasings thereof, have waxed so bold as
to offer new methodologies. It is perhaps symptomatic of
the field's malaise that the suggested cures are a good deal
worse than the disease.[51]

Among the severest critics of Western history are Western
historians themselves. In taking up the cudgels to have at
their own field, they acknowledge its stasis, the intellectual
lethargy of many of its disciples, and its unimaginative and
almost wholly descriptive bent. Insofar as the West, and
particularly the trans-Mississippi West, offers a dramatic
historical landscape wherein individuals and events acquire

[51] See, for example, Seymour V. Connor, "Attitudes and Opinions about
the Mexican War, 1846–1970," *Journal of the West*, Vol. XI (April, 1972), pp.
361–66, and Oliver Knight, "Toward an Understanding of the Western
Town," *The Western Historical Quarterly*, Vol. IV (January, 1973), pp.
27–42. Representative criticisms include W. N. Davis, Jr., "Will the West
Survive as a Field in American History? A Survey Report," *The Mississippi
Valley Historical Review*, Vol. L (March, 1964), pp. 672–85; Earl Pomeroy,
"Toward a Reorientation of Western History: Continuity and Environ-
ment," *ibid.*, Vol. XLI (March, 1955), pp. 579–600; and "The Training of
Western Historians: A Seminar Under the Chairmanship of Walter Rundell,
Jr.," in John Alexander Carroll (ed.), *Reflections of Western Historians*
(Tucson: The University of Arizona Press, 1969), pp. 265–99.

a larger-than-life importance because of their remoteness
from civilization and their isolation from the mainstream
of American culture, Western historians have been pre-
occupied with the dramatic and the exceptional, and few
have sought to add any substantive dimension to their work.
The literature of the field abounds with readable descriptive accounts designed to appeal to audiences more concerned with entertainment than with analysis. Excursions
into theory and method have not been uncommon pastimes
for Western historians, but more often than not, these have
been confined to discussions of Turner's ideas, and then
only as they appear in the 1893 essay. The results of all of
this have been rather more confusing than edifying, if one
assumes that history must have method and meaning. Frequently, however, Western historians have not made that
assumption.[52]

The continuing debate over what Turner said and how
and why he said it has effectively postponed the development in Western historiography of the sort of sophisticated
methodology lately characteristic of other fields of historical
inquiry. This is reflected, in part, in the comfortable ambi-
guity which still allows Western historians to use the terms
"frontier" and "West" interchangeably when in fact the
relationship between them is nebulous at best.[53] Turner, of
course, was interested in the frontier and its effect on an
emerging society. That the American frontier was westward-
moving was wholly coincidental. Yet Turner's work was
used to justify in some academic circles the establishment

[52] See, for example, Clifford M. Drury, "Reminiscences of a Historian,"
The Western Historical Quarterly, Vol. V (April, 1974), p. 148.
[53] For a discussion of the problem, see Jo Tice Bloom, "Cumberland Gap
Versus South Pass: The East or West in Frontier History," *ibid.*, Vol. III
(April, 1972), pp. 153–67.

of the most parochial kind of regional study. There have been other frontiers than one, and Walter Prescott Webb suggested the ramifications of the American frontier experience in a world context in *The Great Frontier*, but since its publication a quarter of a century ago, the book has been studiously ignored by most Western historians.[54] This is hardly surprising, given the prevailing intellectual construct of Western history, a construct that permits elaborate and protracted discussions of Turner's rhetoric and leaves substantive studies of the frontier as a focal point for social, political, and economic change to anthropologists and geographers.

"The principal failing of Turner, his followers, and most of his critics," geographer Marvin W. Mikesell has observed, "has been a neglect of comparative research. Without a perspective afforded by knowledge of developments in foreign areas, it is not possible to interpret the significance of the American frontier."[55] Turner's critics, as well as his advocates, have of course been concerned with testing the validity of the 1893 "hypothesis." The critics have embraced a superficial comparative methodology to demonstrate that Turner's ideas have little application to other frontiers in other parts of the world and thereby to damn them. Advocates who thus find neither aid nor comfort in the comparative approach have naturally avoided it.[56] Again,

[54] Walter Prescott Webb, *The Great Frontier* (New ed., Austin: University of Texas Press, 1964).

[55] Marvin W. Mikesell, "Comparative Studies in Frontier History," *Annals of the Association of American Geographers*, Vol. 50 (March, 1960), p. 64.

[56] For a discussion, see Ray Allen Billington, "Frontiers," in C. Vann Woodward (ed.), *The Comparative Approach to American History* (New York: Basic Books, Inc., 1968), pp. 75–90; and Paul F. Sharp, "Three Frontiers: Some Comparative Studies of Canadian, American, and Australian

the problem of the frontier seems less important than tenuous discussions of Turner's dicta.

Turner himself, as we have seen, did not neglect comparative research, and Mikesell's reading of Turner must stand as a cursory one in this respect. The first few pages of the dissertation here reprinted indicate that comparative history was not unknown to Turner, a point further substantiated by the institutional orientation apparent in much of his writing. But beyond that, here is yet another example of Turner's work being put to a use for which it was not intended. Turner wrote of the impact of the frontier on American development, and he did so acknowledging its importance to the study of European history from a colonial perspective. He treated the frontier in this case as an isolated rather than a general phenomenon, which is the geographer's concern. His interest was not in what America revealed about frontiers but what one frontier suggested about America. The important work of examining frontiers in the context of comparative research must indeed be done, but there is little to be gained by prefacing such a project with the flagellation of a man who was concerned with other matters.

The misapprehension of Turner's work by those involved with the study of the universal aspects of frontier phenomena certainly does not lessen the validity of their criticisms of the aimlessness of Western history. Rather, it amplifies the need for the kind of interdisciplinary research that Turner himself advocated.[57] If Western history is to escape from the morass of parochialism in which it is mired, its

Settlement," *The Pacific Historical Review*, Vol. XXIV (November, 1955), pp. 369–77.

[57] Billington, *Frederick Jackson Turner*, pp. 493–97.

practitioners might well embrace comparative frontier research and acquire what anthropologists and geographers
have to offer in the way of theory and method.[58] There is
no need to find in Turner's writing a starting point (a suggestion, it could be argued, that other social scientists might
do well to accept), but it is obligatory that, whatever use is
made of his work, it must be considered for what it was and
not distorted to accommodate schema that, for whatever
reason, may be currently fashionable. If Western historians
continue to look to Turner for guidance, it must be with a
fresh understanding of the task he was about, a task amply
demonstrated by his dissertation. And they must acquire the
flexibility of mind and the breadth of interest that allows
them to perceive, as he did, the interconnection between
histories as diverse as those of Phoenician merchants and
American fur traders. Otherwise, the field of historical
inquiry most closely linked with Turner's name will bear
the least relationship to the work he did and will remain
the stepchild of the profession.

[58] See Gene M. Gressley, "Land and Man in Monaro, El Paso, and
Denver," *Agricultural History*, Vol. XLVIII (July, 1974), 441–49, and D. W.
Meinig, "American Wests: Preface to a Geographical Interpretation," *Annals
of the Association of American Geographers*, Vol. 62 (June, 1972), pp. 159–84.
Of interest also is the entire issue of *Papers in Anthropology*, Vol. 14
(Spring, 1973), which is devoted to various aspects of pioneer colonization
of frontier areas.

THE CHARACTER AND INFLUENCE OF THE
INDIAN TRADE IN WISCONSIN

*"The history of commerce is the history of the intercom-
munication of peoples."*—MONTESQUIEU.

I.

~~~~~~

INTRODUCTION[1]

The trading post is an old and influential institution. Established in the midst of an undeveloped society by a more advanced people, it is a center not only of new economic influences, but also of all the transforming forces that accompany the intercourse of a higher with a lower civilization. The Phœnicians developed the institution into a great his-

---

[1] In this paper I have rewritten and enlarged an address before the State Historical Society of Wisconsin on the Character and Influence of the Fur Trade in Wisconsin, published in the Proceedings of the Thirty-sixth Annual Meeting, 1889. I am under obligations to Mr. Reuben G. Thwaites, Secretary of this society, for his generous assistance in procuring material for my work, and to Professor Charles H. Haskins, my colleague, who kindly read both manuscript and proof and made helpful suggestions. The reader will notice that throughout the paper I have used the word *Northwest* in a limited sense as referring to the region included between the Great Lakes and the Ohio and Mississippi rivers.

[Editors' Note: Turner's footnotes have been renumbered for the convenience of the reader, and in some instances page references have been clarified. Otherwise, the text is as it originally appeared. Organizational discrepancies in table of contents and text have been resolved. As published by Johns Hopkins University, the dissertation contained no bibliography. We have prepared a new index for this edition.]

toric agency. Closely associated with piracy at first, their commerce gradually freed itself from this and spread throughout the Mediterranean lands. A passage in the Odyssey (Book XV) enables us to trace the genesis of the Phœnician trading post:

> "Thither came the Phœnicians, mariners renowned, greedy merchant-men with countless trinkets in a black ship . . . . They abode among us a whole year, and got together much wealth in their hollow ship. And when their hollow ship was now laden to depart, they sent a messenger . . . . There came a man versed in craft to my father's house with a golden chain strung here and there with amber beads. Now, the maidens in the hall and my lady mother were handling the chain and gazing on it and offering him their price."

It would appear that the traders at first sailed from port to port, bartering as they went. After a time they stayed at certain profitable places a twelvemonth, still trading from their ships. Then came the fixed factory, and about it grew the trading colony.[2] The Phœnician trading post wove together the fabric of oriental civilization, brought arts and the alphabet to Greece, brought the elements of civilization to northern Africa, and disseminated eastern culture through the Mediterranean system of lands. It blended races and customs, developed commercial confidence, fostered the custom of depending on outside nations for certain supplies, and afforded a means of peaceful intercourse between societies naturally hostile.

Carthaginian, Greek, Etruscan and Roman trading posts continued the process. By traffic in amber, tin, furs, etc., with the tribes of the north of Europe, a continental com-

2 On the trading colony, see Roscher und Jannasch, Colonien, p. 12.

4

merce was developed. The routes of this trade have been ascertained.[3] For over a thousand years before the migration of the peoples Mediterranean commerce had flowed along the interlacing river valleys of Europe, and trading posts had been established. Museums show how important an effect was produced upon the economic life of northern Europe by this intercourse. It is a significant fact that the routes of the migration of the peoples were to a considerable extent the routes of Roman trade, and it is well worth inquiry whether this commerce did not leave more traces upon Teutonic society than we have heretofore considered, and whether one cause of the migrations of the peoples has not been neglected.[4]

That stage in the development of society when a primitive people comes into contact with a more advanced people deserves more study than has been given to it. As a factor in breaking the "cake of custom" the meeting of two such societies is of great importance; and if, with Starcke,[5] we trace the origin of the family to economic considerations, and, with Schrader,[6] the institution of guest friendship to the same source, we may certainly expect to find important influences upon primitive society arising from commerce with a higher people. The extent to which such commerce

[3] Consult: Müllenhoff, Altertumskunde, I., p. 212; Schrader, Prehistoric Antiquities of the Aryan Peoples, New York, 1890, pp. 348ff.; Pliny, Naturalis Historia, xxvii., p. 11; Montelius, Civilization of Sweden in Heathen Times, 98–99; Du Chaillu, Viking Age; and the citations in Dawkins, Early Man in Britain, 466–67; Keary, Vikings, in Western Christendom, 23.

[4] In illustration it may be noted that the early Scandinavian power in Russia seized upon the trade route by the Dnieper and the Duna. Keary, Vikings, p. 173. See also post, pp. 40–43.

[5] Starcke, Primitive Family.

[6] Schrader, p. 1. c.; see also Ihring, in Deutsche Rundschau, III., pp. 357, 420; Kulischer, Der Handel auf primitiven Kulturstufen, in Zeitschrift für Völkerpsychologie und Sprachwissenschaft, X., p. 378. Vide post, p. 8.

has affected all peoples is remarkable. One may study the process from the days of Phœnicia to the days of England in Africa,[7] but nowhere is the material more abundant than in the history of the relations of the Europeans and the American Indians. The Phœnician factory, it is true, fostered the development of the Mediterranean civilization, while in America the trading post exploited the natives. The explanation of this difference is to be sought partly in race differences, partly in the greater gulf that separated the civilization of the European from the civilization of the American Indian as compared with that which parted the early Greeks and the Phœnicians. But the study of the destructive effect of the trading post is valuable as well as the study of its elevating influences; in both cases the effects are important and worth investigation and comparison.

[7] W. Bosworth Smith, in a suggestive article in the *Nineteenth Century*, December, 1887, shows the influence of the Mohammedan trade in Africa.

II.

⚬⚬⚬⚬⚬⚬⚬⚬⚬⚬⚬⚬⚬⚬⚬⚬⚬⚬⚬⚬⚬⚬⚬⚬⚬⚬⚬⚬⚬⚬

PRIMITIVE INTER-TRIBAL TRADE

Long before the advent of the white trader, inter-tribal commercial intercourse existed. Mr. Charles Rau[1] and Sir Daniel Wilson[2] have shown that inter-tribal trade and division of labor were common among the mound-builders and in the stone age generally. In historic times there is ample evidence of inter-tribal trade. Were positive evidence lacking, Indian institutions would disclose the fact. Differences in language were obviated by the sign language,[3] a fixed system of communication, intelligible to all the western tribes at least. The peace pipe,[4] or calumet, was used for settling disputes, strengthening alliances, and speaking to strangers—a sanctity attached to it. Wampum belts served in New England and the middle region as money and as

[1] Smithsonian Report, 1872.

[2] Transactions of the Royal Society of Canada, 1889, VII., p. 59. See also Thruston, Antiquities of Tennessee, p. 79ff.

[3] Mallery, in Bureau of Ethnology, I., p. 324; Clark, Indian Sign Language.

[4] Shea, Discovery of the Mississippi, p. 34. Catilinite pipes were widely used, even along the Atlantic slope, Thruston, pp. 80–81.

7

symbols in the ratification of treaties.[5] The Chippeways had an institution called by a term signifying "to enter one another's lodges,"[6] whereby a truce was made between them and the Sioux at the winter hunting season. During these seasons of peace it was not uncommon for a member of one tribe to adopt a member of another as his brother, a tie which was respected even after the expiration of the truce. The analogy of this custom to the classical "guest-friendship" needs no comment; and the economic cause of the institution is worth remark, as one of the means by which the rigor of primitive inter-tribal hostility was mitigated.

But it is not necessary to depend upon indirect evidence. The earliest travellers testify to the existence of a wide intertribal commerce. The historians of De Soto's expedition mention Indian merchants who sold salt to the inland tribes. "In 1565 and for some years previous bison skins were brought by the Indians down the Potomac, and thence carried along-shore in canoes to the French about the Gulf of St. Lawrence. During the two years six thousand skins were thus obtained."[7] An Algonquin brought to Champlain at Quebec a piece of copper a foot long, which he said came from a tributary of the Great Lakes.[8] Champlain also reports that among the Canadian Indians village councils were held to determine what number of men might go to trade with other tribes in the summer.[9] Morton in 1632 describes similar inter-tribal trade in New England, and adds that certain utensils are "but in certain parts of the country made, where the severall trades are appropriated to the

5 Weeden, Economic and Social History of New England, I., ch. ii.

6 Minnesota Historical Collections, V., p. 267.

7 Parkman, Pioneers of France in the New World, p. 230, citing Menendez.

8 Neill, in Narrative and Critical History of America, IV., p. 164.

9 Champlain's Voyages (Prince Society), III., p. 183.

inhabitants of those parts onely."[10] Marquette relates that the Illinois bought firearms of the Indians who traded directly wth the French, and that they went to the south and west to carry off slaves, which they sold at a high price to other nations.[11] It was on the foundation, therefore, of an extensive inter-tribal trade that the white man built up the forest commerce.[12]

[10] Morton, New English Canaan (Prince Society), p. 159.
[11] Shea, Discovery and Exploration of the Mississippi Valley, p. 32.
[12] For additional evidence see Radisson, Voyages (Prince Society), p. 91, 173; Massachusetts Historical Collections, I., p. 151; Smithsonian Contributions, XVI., p. 30; Jesuit Relations, 1671, p. 41; Thruston, Antiquities, etc., pp. 79–82; Carr, Mounds of the Mississippi Valley, pp. 25, 27; and *post* pp. 29–30, 41.

III.

PLACE OF THE INDIAN TRADE IN THE SETTLEMENT OF AMERICA

1. EARLY TRADE ALONG THE ATLANTIC COAST

The chroniclers of the earliest voyages to the Atlantic coast abound in references to this traffic. First of Europeans to purchase native furs in America appear to have been the Norsemen who settled Vinland. In the saga of Eric the Red[1] we find this interesting account: "Thereupon Karlsefni and his people displayed their shields, and when they came together they began to barter with each other. Especially did the strangers wish to buy red cloth, for which they offered in exchange peltries and quite grey skins. They also desired to buy swords and spears, but Karlsefni and Snorri forbade this. In exchange for perfect unsullied skins the Skrellings would take red stuff a span in length, which they would bind around their heads. So their trade went on for a time, until Karlsefni and his people began to grow short of cloth, when they divided it into such pieces that it was not

---

[1] Reeves, Finding of Wineland the Good, p. 47.

11

more than a finger's breadth wide, but the Skrellings still continued to give just as much for this as before, or more."

The account of Verrazano's voyage[2] mentions his Indian trade. Captain John Smith, exploring New England in 1614, brought back a cargo of fish and 11,000 beaver skins.[3] These examples could be multiplied; in short, a way was prepared for colonization by the creation of a demand for European goods, and thus the opportunity for a lodgement was afforded.

2. NEW ENGLAND INDIAN TRADE

The Indian trade has a place in the early history of the New England colonies. The Plymouth settlers "found divers corn fields and little running brooks, a place . . . fit for situation,"[4] and settled down cuckoo-like in Indian clearings. Mr. Weeden has shown that the Indian trade furnished a currency (wampum) to New England, and that it afforded the beginnings of her commerce. In September of their first year the Plymouth men sent out a shallop to trade with the Indians, and when a ship arrived from England in 1621 they speedily loaded her with a return cargo of beaver and lumber.[5] By frequent legislation the colonies regulated and fostered the trade.[6] Bradford reports that in

[2] N. Y. Hist. Colls., I., pp. 54–55, 59.

[3] Smith, Generall Historie (Richmond, 1819), I., pp. 87–88, 182, 199; Strachey's Travaile into Virginia, p. 157 (Hakluyt Soc. VI.); Parkman, Pioneers, p. 230.

[4] Bradford, Plymouth Plantation.

[5] Bradford, 104.

[6] E. g., Plymouth Records, I., pp. 50, 54, 62, 119; II., p. 10; Massachusetts Colonial Records, I., pp. 55, 81, 96, 100, 322; II., pp. 86, 138; III., p. 424; V., p. 180; Hazard, Historical Collections, II., p. 19 (the Commissioners of the United Colonies propose giving the monopoly of the fur trade to a corporation). On public truck-houses, vide post, p. 66.

a single year twenty hhd. of furs were shipped from Plymouth, and that between 1631 and 1636 their shipments amounted to 12,150 *li.* beaver and 1156 *li.* otter.[7] Morton in his 'New English Canaan' alleges that a servant of his was "thought to have a thousand pounds in ready gold gotten by the beaver when he died."[8] In the pursuit of this trade men passed continually farther into the wilderness, and their trading posts "generally became the pioneers of new settlements."[9] For example, the posts of Oldham, a Puritan trader, led the way for the settlements on the Connecticut river,[10] and in their early days these towns were partly sustained by the Indian trade.[11]

Not only did the New England traders expel the Dutch from this valley; they contended with them on the Hudson.[12]

3. INDIAN TRADE IN THE MIDDLE COLONIES

Morton, in the work already referred to, protested against allowing "the Great Lake of the Erocoise" (Champlain) to the Dutch, saying that it is excellent for the fur trade, and that the Dutch have gained by beaver 20,000 pounds a year. Exaggerated though the statement is, it is true that the energies of the Dutch were devoted to this trade, rather than to agricultural settlement. As in the case of New France the settlers dispersed themselves in the Indian trade; so general did this become that laws had to be passed to

[7] Bradford, p. 108, gives the proceeds of the sale of these furs.
[8] Force, Collections, Vol. I., No. 5, p. 53.
[9] Weeden, I., pp. 132, 160-61.
[10] Winthrop, History of New England, I., pp. 111, 131.
[11] Connecticut Colonial Records, 1637, pp. 11, 18.
[12] Weeden, I., p. 126.

compel the raising of crops.[13] New York City (New Amsterdam) was founded and for a time sustained by the fur trade. In their search for peltries the Dutch were drawn up the Hudson, up the Connecticut, and down the Delaware, where they had Swedes for their rivals. By way of the Hudson the Dutch traders had access to Lake Champlain, and to the Mohawk, the headwaters of which connected through the lakes of western New York with Lake Ontario. This region, which was supplied by the trading post of Orange (Albany), was the seat of the Iroquois confederacy. The results of the trade upon Indian society became apparent in a short time in the most decisive way. Furnished with arms by the Dutch, the Iroquois turned upon the neighboring Indians, whom the French had at first refrained from supplying with guns.[14] In 1649 they completely ruined the Hurons,[15] a part of whom fled to the woods of northern Wisconsin. In the years immediately following, the Neutral Nation and the Eries fell under their power; they overawed the New England Indians and the Southern tribes, and their hunting and war parties visited Illinois and drove Indians of those plains into Wisconsin. Thus by priority in securing firearms, as well as by their remarkable civil organization,[16] the Iroquois secured possession of the St. Lawrence and Lakes Ontario and Erie. The French had accepted the alliance of the Algonquins and the Hurons, as the Dutch, and afterward the English, had that of the Iroquois; so these victories of the Iroquois cut the French off from the entrance

13 New York Colonial Documents, I., pp. 181, 389, §7.
14 *Ibid.* 182; Collection de manuscrits relatifs à la Nouvelle-France, I., p. 254; Radisson, p. 93.
15 Parkman, Jesuits in North America; Radisson; Margry, Découvertes et Établissements, etc., IV., pp. 586–98; Tailhan, Nicholas Perrot.
16 Morgan, League of the Iroquois.

to the Great Lakes by way of the upper St. Lawrence. As early as 1629 the Dutch trade was estimated at 50,000 guilders per annum, and the Delaware trade alone produced 10,000 skins yearly in 1663.[17] The English succeeded to this trade, and under Governor Dongan they made particular efforts to extend their operations to the Northwest, using the Iroquois as middlemen. Although the French were in possession of the trade with the Algonquins of the Northwest, the English had an economic advantage in competing for this trade in the fact that Albany traders, whose situation enabled them to import their goods more easily than Montreal traders could, and who were burdened with fewer governmental restrictions, were able to pay fifty per cent more for beaver and give better goods. French traders frequently received their supplies from Albany, a practice against which the English authorities legislated in 1720; and the *coureurs de bois* smuggled their furs to the same place.[18] As early as 1666 Talon proposed that the king of France should purchase New York, "whereby he would have two entrances to Canada and by which he would give to the French all the peltries of the north, of which the English share the profit by the communication which they have with the Iroquois by Manhattan and Orange."[19] It is a characteristic of the fur trade that it continually recedes from the original center, and so it happened that the English traders before long attempted to work their way into the Illinois country. The wars between the French and English and

17 N. Y. Col. Docs., IX., pp. 408–409; V., pp. 687, 726; Histoire et Commerce des Colonies Angloises, p. 154.

18 N. Y. Col. Docs., III., pp. 471, 474; IX., pp. 298, 319.

19 *Ibid.* IX., p. 57. The same proposal was made in 1681 by Du Chesneau, *ibid.* IX., p. 165.

Iroquois must be read in the light of this fact.[20] At the out-break of the last French and Indian war, however, it was rather Pennsylvania and Virginia traders who visited the Ohio Valley. It is said that some three hundred of them came over the mountains yearly, following the Susquehanna and the Juniata and the headwaters of the Potomac to the tributaries of the Ohio, and visiting with their pack-horses the Indian villages along the valley. The center of the English trade was Pickawillani on the Great Miami. In 1749 Celoron de Bienville, who had been sent out to vindicate French authority in the valley, reported that each village along the Ohio and its branches "has one or more English traders, and each of these has hired men to carry his furs."[21]

4. Indian Trade in the Southern Colonies

The Indian trade of the Virginians was not limited to the Ohio country. As in the case of Massachusetts Bay, the trade had been provided for before the colony left England,[22] and in times of need it had preserved the infant settlement. Bacon's rebellion was in part due to the opposition to the governor's trading relations with the savages. After a time the nearer Indians were exploited, and as early as the close of the seventeenth century Virginia traders sought the Indi-ans west of the Alleghanies.[23] The Cherokees lived among

20 Parkman's works; N. Y. Col. Docs., IX., p. 165; Shea's Charlevoix, IV., p. 16; "The English, indeed, as already remarked, from that time shared with the French in the fur trade; and this was the chief motive of their fomenting war between us and the Iroquois, inasmuch as they could get no good furs, which come from the northern districts, except by means of these Indians, who could scarcely effect a reconciliation with us without precluding them from this precious mine."
21 Parkman, Montcalm and Wolfe, I., p. 50.
22 Charter of 1606.
23 Ramsay, Tennessee, p. 63.

16

the mountains, "where the present states of Tennessee, Alabama, Georgia, and the Carolinas join one another."[24] To the west, on the Mississippi, were the Chickasaws, south of whom lived the Choctaws, while to the south of the Cherokees were the Creeks. The Catawbas had their villages on the border of North and South Carolina, about the headwaters of the Santee river. Shawnese Indians had formerly lived on the Cumberland river, and French traders had been among them, as well as along the Mississippi;[25] but by the time of the English traders, Tennessee and Kentucky were for the most part uninhabited. The Virginia traders reached the Catawbas, and for a time the Cherokees, by a trading route through the southwest of the colony to the Santee. By 1712 this trade was a well-established one,[26] and the caravans of one hundred pack-horses passed along the trail.[27]

The Carolinas had early been interested in the fur trade. In 1663 the Lords Proprietors proposed to pay the governor's salary from the proceeds of the traffic. Charleston traders were the rivals of the Virginians in the southwest. They passed even to the Choctaws and Chickasaws, crossing the rivers by portable boats of skin, and sometimes taking up a permanent abode among the Indians. Virginia and Carolina traders were not on good terms with each other, and Governor Spottswood frequently made complaints of the actions of the Carolinians. His expedition across the mountains in 1716, if his statement is to be trusted, opened a new way to the transmontane Indians, and soon afterwards

[24] On the Southwestern Indians see Adair, American Indians.
[25] Ramsay, p. 75.
[26] Spottswood's Letters, Virginia Hist. Colls., N. S., I., p. 67.
[27] Byrd Manuscripts, I., p. 180. The reader will find a convenient map for the southern region in Roosevelt, Winning of the West, I.

a trading company was formed under his patronage to avail themselves of this new route.[28] It passed across the Blue Ridge into the Shenandoah valley, and down the old Indian trail to the Cherokees, who lived along the upper Tennessee. Below the bend at the Muscle Shoals the Virginians met the competition of the French traders from New Orleans and Mobile.[29]

The settlement of Augusta, Georgia, was another important trading post. Here in 1740 was an English garrison of fifteen or twenty soldiers, and a little band of traders, who annually took about five hundred pack-horses into the Indian country. In the spring the furs were floated down the river in large boats.[30] The Spaniards and the French also visited the Indians, and the rivalry over this trade was an important factor in causing diplomatic embroilment.[31]

The occupation of the back-lands of the South affords a prototype of the process by which the plains of the far West were settled, and also furnishes an exemplification of all the stages of economic development existing contemporaneously. After a time the traders were accompanied to the Indian ground by *hunters*, and sometimes the two callings were combined.[32] When Boone entered Kentucky he went with an Indian trader whose posts were on the Red river in Kentucky.[33] After the game decreased the hunter's clearing was occupied by the *cattle-raiser*, and his home, as settlement grew, became the property of the *cultivator of the soil*;[34] the *manufacturing era* belongs to our own time.

28 Spottswood's Letters, I., 40; II., pp. 149, 150.
29 Ramsay, p. 64. Note the bearing of this route on the Holston settlement.
30 Georgia Historical Collections, I., p. 180; II., pp. 123–27.
31 Spottswood, II., p. 131, for example.
32 Ramsay, p. 65.
33 Boone, Life and Adventures.
34 Observations on the North American Land Co., pp. xv., 144, London, 1796.

5. INDIAN TRADE IN THE FAR WEST

In the South, the Middle Colonies and New England the trade opened the water-courses, the trading post grew into the palisaded town, and rival nations sought to possess the trade for themselves. Throughout the colonial frontier the effect, as well as the methods, of Indian traffic were strikingly alike. The trader was the pathfinder for civilization. Nor was the process limited to the east of the Mississippi. The expeditions of Verenderye led to the discovery of the Rocky Mountains.[35] French traders passed up the Missouri; and when the Lewis and Clarke expedition ascended that river and crossed the continent, it went with traders and voyageurs as guides and interpreters. Indeed, Jefferson first conceived the idea of such an expedition[36] from contact with Ledyard, who was organizing a fur trading company in France, and it was proposed to Congress as a means of fostering our western Indian trade.[37] The first immigrant train to California was incited by the representations of an Indian trader who had visited the region, and it was guided by trappers.[38]

St. Louis was the center of the fur trade of the far West, and Senator Benton was intimate with leading traders like Chouteau.[39] He urged the occupation of the Oregon country, where in 1810 an establishment had for a time been made by the celebrated John Jacob Astor; and he fostered legislation opening the road to the southwestern Mexican settlements long in use by the traders. The expedition of

[35] Margry, VI.
[36] Allen, Lewis and Clarke Expedition, I., p. ix.; *vide post*, pp. 80–81.
[37] *Vide post*, p. 81.
[38] *Century Magazine*, XLI., p. 759.
[39] Jessie Benton Frémont in *Century Magazine*, XLI., pp. 766–67.

his son-in-law Frémont was made with French voyageurs, and guided to the passes by traders who had used them before.[40] Benton was also one of the stoutest of the early advocates of a Pacific railway.

But the Northwest[41] was particularly the home of the fur trade, and having seen that this traffic was not an isolated or unimportant matter, we may now proceed to study it in detail with Wisconsin as the field of investigation.

[40] *Century Magazine*, XLI., p. 759; *vide post*, p. 84.

[41] Parkman's works, particularly Old Régime, make any discussion of the importance of the fur trade to Canada proper unnecessary. La Hontan says: "For you must know that Canada subsists only upon the trade of skins or furs, three-fourths of which come from the people that live around the Great Lakes." La Hontan, I., p. 53, London, 1703.

IV.

~~~~~~

THE RIVER AND LAKE SYSTEMS OF
THE NORTHWEST

The importance of physical conditions is nowhere more manifest than in the exploration of the Northwest, and we cannot properly appreciate Wisconsin's relation to the history of the time without first considering her situation as regards the lake and river systems of North America.

When the Breton sailors, steering their fishing smacks almost in the wake of Cabot, began to fish in the St. Lawrence gulf, and to traffic with the natives of the mainland for peltries, the problem of how the interior of North America was to be explored was solved. The water-system composed of the St. Lawrence and the Great Lakes is the key to the continent. The early explorations in a wilderness must be by water-courses—they are nature's highways. The St. Lawrence leads to the Great Lakes; the headwaters of the tributaries of these lakes lie so near the headwaters of the rivers that join the Mississippi that canoes can be portaged from the one to the other. The Mississippi affords passage to the Gulf of Mexico; or by the Missouri to the passes of the Rocky Mountains, where rise the headwaters of the Columbia, which brings the voyageur to the Pacific. But if the explorer follows Lake Superior to the present boundary line between Minnesota and Canada, and takes the chain of lakes and rivers extending from Pigeon river to Rainy lake and Lake of the Woods, he will be led to the Winnipeg river and to the lake of the same name. From this, by streams and portages, he may reach Hudson bay; or he may go by way of Elk river and Lake Athabasca to Slave river and Slave lake, which will take him to Mackenzie river and to the Arctic sea. But Lake Winnipeg also receives the waters of the Saskatchewan river, from which one may pass to the highlands near the Pacific where rise the northern branches of the Columbia. And from the lakes of Canada there are still other routes to the Oregon country.[1] At a later day these two routes to the Columbia became an important factor in bringing British and Americans into conflict over that territory.

In these water-systems Wisconsin was the link that joined the Great Lakes and the Mississippi; and along her northern shore the first explorers passed to the Pigeon river, or, as it was called later, the Grand Portage route, along the boundary line between Minnesota and Canada into the heart of Canada.

It was possible to reach the Mississippi from the Great Lakes by the following principal routes:[2]

1. By the Miami (Maumee) river from the west end of Lake Erie to the Wabash, thence to the Ohio and the Mississippi.

[1] Narr. and Crit. Hist. Amer., VIII., pp. 10–11.
[2] Narr. and Crit. Hist. Amer., IV., p. 224, n. 1; Margry, V. See also Parkman, Montcalm and Wolfe, I., map and pp. 38–39, 128.

2. By the St. Joseph's river to the Wabash, thence to the Ohio.

3. By the St. Joseph's river to the Kankakee, and thence to the Illinois and the Mississippi.

4. By the Chicago river to the Illinois.

5. By Green bay, Fox river, and the Wisconsin river.

6. By the Bois Brulé river to the St. Croix river.

Of these routes, the first two were not at first available, owing to the hostility of the Iroquois.

Of all the colonies that fell to the English, as we have seen, New York alone had a water-system that favored communication with the interior, tapping the St. Lawrence and opening a way to Lake Ontario. Prevented by the Iroquois friends of the Dutch and English from reaching the Northwest by way of the lower lakes, the French ascended the Ottawa, reached Lake Nipissing, and passed by way of Georgian Bay to the islands of Lake Huron. As late as the nineteenth century this was the common route of the fur trade, for it was more certain for the birch canoes than the tempestuous route of the lakes. At the Huron islands two ways opened before their canoes. The straits of Michillimackinac[3] permitted them to enter Lake Michigan, and from this led the two routes to the Mississippi: one by way of Green bay and the Fox and Wisconsin, and the other by way of the lake to the Chicago river. But if the trader chose to go from the Huron islands through Sault Ste. Marie into Lake Superior, the necessities of his frail craft required him to hug the shore, and the rumors of copper mines induced the first traders to take the south shore, and here the lakes of northern Wisconsin and Minnesota afford connecting links between the streams that seek Lake Superior and those

3 Mackinaw.

that seek the Mississippi,[4] a fact which made northern Wisconsin more important in this epoch than the southern portion of the state.

We are now able to see how the river-courses of the Northwest permitted a complete exploration of the country, and that in these courses Wisconsin held a commanding situation.[5] But these rivers not only permitted exploration; they also furnished a motive to exploration by the fact that their valleys teemed with fur-bearing animals. This is the main fact in connection with Northwestern exploration. The hope of a route to China was always influential, as was also the search for mines, but the practical inducements were the profitable trade with the Indians for beaver and buffaloes and the wild life that accompanied it. So powerful was the combined influence of these far-stretching rivers, and the "hardy, adventurous, lawless, fascinating fur trade," that the scanty population of Canada was irresistibly drawn from agricultural settlements into the interminable recesses of the continent; and herein is a leading explanation of the lack of permanent French influence in America.

4 See Doty's enumeration, Wis. Hist. Colls., VII., p. 202.
5 Jes. Rels., 1672, p. 37; La Hontan, I., p. 105 (1703).

V.

~~~~~~

WISCONSIN INDIANS[1]

"All that relates to the Indian tribes of Wisconsin," says Dr. Shea, "their antiquities, their ethnology, their history, is deeply interesting from the fact that it is the area of the first meeting of the Algic and Dakota tribes. Here clans of both these wide-spread families met and mingled at a very early period; here they first met in battle and mutually checked each other's advance." The Winnebagoes attracted the attention of the French even before they were visited. They were located about Green bay. Their later location at the entrance of Lake Winnebago was unoccupied, at least in the time of Allouez, because of the hostility of the Sioux. Early authorities represented them as numbering about one hundred warriors.[2] The Pottawattomies we find in 1641

[1] On these early locations, consult the authorities cited by Shea in Wis. Hist. Colls., III., p. 125 *et seq.*, and by Brunson in his criticism on Shea, *ibid.* IV., p. 223. See also Butterfield's Discovery of the Northwest in 1634, and *Mag. West. Hist.*, V., pp. 468, 630; and Minn. Hist. Colls., V.

[2] Some early estimates were as follows: 1640, "Great numbers" (Margry, I., p. 48); 1718, 80 to 100 warriors (N. Y. Col. Docs., IX., p. 889); 1728, 60 or

at Sault Ste. Marie,[3] whither they had just fled from their enemies. Their proper home was probably about the southeastern shore and islands of Green bay, where as early as 1670 they were again located. Of their numbers in Wisconsin at this time we can say but little. Allouez, at Chequamegon bay, was visited by 300 of their warriors, and he mentions some of their Green bay villages, one of which had 300 souls.[4] The Menomonees were found chiefly on the river that bears their name, and the western tributaries of Green bay seem to have been their territory. On the estimates of early authorities we may say that they had about 100 warriors.[5] The Sauks and Foxes were closely allied tribes. The Sauks were found by Allouez[6] four leagues[7] up the Fox from its mouth, and the Foxes at a place reached by a four days' ascent of the Wolf river from its mouth. Later we find them at the confluence of the Wolf and the Fox. According to their early visitors these two tribes must have had something over 1000 warriors.[8] The Miamis and Mascoutins were located about a league from the Fox river, probably within the limits of what is now Green Lake

---

80 warriors (Margry, VI., p. 553); 1736, 90 warriors (Chaurignerie, cited in Schoolcraft's Indian Tribes, III., p. 282); 1761, 150 warriors (Gorrell, Wis. Hist. Colls., I., p. 32).

[3] Margry, I., p. 46.

[4] Jes. Rels., 1667, 1670.

[5] 1718, estimated at 80 to 100 warriors (N. Y. Col. Docs., IX., p. 889); 1762, estimated at 150 warriors (Gorrell, Wis. Hist. Colls., I., p. 32).

[6] Jes. Rels., 1670.

[7] French leagues.

[8] 1670, Foxes estimated at 400 warriors (Jes. Rels., 1670); 1667, Foxes, 1000 warriors (Jes. Rels., 1667); 1695, Foxes and Mascoutins, 1200 warriors (N. Y. Col. Doc., IX., p. 633); 1718, Sauks 100 or 120, Foxes 500 warriors (2 Penn. Archives, VI., p. 54); 1728, Foxes, 200 warriors (Margry, V.); 1762, Sauks and Foxes, 700 warriors (Gorrell, Wis. Hist. Colls., I., p. 32). This, it must be observed, was after the Fox wars.

county,[9] and four leagues away were their friends the Kick-apoos. In 1670 the Miamis and Mascoutins were estimated at 800 warriors, and this may have included the Kickapoos. The Sioux held possession of the Upper Mississippi, and in Wisconsin hunted on its northeastern tributaries. Their villages were in later times all on the west of the Mississippi, and of their early numbers no estimate can be given. The Chippeways were along the southern shore of Lake Superior. Their numbers also are in doubt, but were very considerable.[10] In northwestern Wisconsin, with Chequamegon bay as their rendezvous, were the Ottawas and Hurons,[11] who had fled here to escape the Iroquois. In 1670 they were back again to their homes at Mackinaw and the Huron islands. But in 1666, as Allouez tells us, they were situated at the bottom of this beautiful bay, planting their Indian corn and leading a stationary life. "They are there," he says, "to the number of eight hundred men bearing arms, but collected from seven different nations who dwell in peace with each other thus mingled together."[12] And the Jesuit Relations of 1670 add that the Illinois "come here from time to time in great numbers as merchants to procure hatchets, cooking utensils, guns, and other things of which they stand in need." Here, too, came Pottawattomies, as we have seen, and Sauks.

At the mouth of Fox river[13] we find another mixed village of Pottawattomies, Sauks, Foxes, and Winnebagoes, and at

9 Jes. Rels., 1670; Butterfield's Discovery of the Northwest.

10 In 1820 those in Wisconsin numbered about 600 hunters.

11 On these Indians consult, besides authorities already cited, Shea's Discovery, etc. lx.; Jes. Rels.; Narr. and Crit. Hist. of Amer., IV., pp. 168–70, 175; Radisson's Voyages; Margry, IV., pp. 586–98.

12 Jes. Rels., 1666–67.

13 Jes. Rels., 1670.

a later period Milwaukee was the site of a similar hetero-geneous community. Leaving out the Hurons, the tribes of Wisconsin were, with two exceptions, of the Algic stock. The exceptions are the Winnebagoes and the Sioux, who belong to the Dakota family. Of these Wisconsin tribes it is probable that the Sauks and Foxes, the Pottawattomies, the Hurons and Ottawas and the Mascoutins, and Miamis and Kickapoos, were driven into Wisconsin by the attacks of eastern enemies. The Iroquois even made incursions as far as the home of the Mascoutins on Fox river. On the other side of the state were the Sioux, "the Iroquois of the West," as the missionaries call them, who had once claimed all the regions, and whose invasions, Allouez says, rendered Lake Winnebago uninhabited. There was therefore a pressure on both sides of Wisconsin which tended to mass together the divergent tribes. And the Green bay and Fox and Wis-consin route was the line of least resistance, as well as a region abounding in wild rice, fish and game, for these early fugitives. In this movement we have two facts that are not devoid of significance in institutional history: first, the welding together of separate tribes, as the Sauks and Foxes, and the Miamis, Mascoutins and Kickapoos; and second, a commingling of detached families from various tribes at peculiarly favorable localities.

VI.

~~~~~~

PERIODS OF THE WISCONSIN INDIAN TRADE

The Indian trade was almost the sole interest in Wisconsin during the two centuries that elapsed from the visit of Nicolet in 1634 to about 1834, when lead-mining had superseded it in the southwest and land offices were opened at Green Bay and Mineral Point; when the port of Milwaukee received an influx of settlers to the lands made known by the so-called Black Hawk war; and when Astor retired from the American Fur Company. These two centuries may be divided into three periods of the trade: 1. French, from 1634 to 1763; 2. English, from 1763 to 1816; 3. American, from 1816 to 1834.

1. FRENCH EXPLORATION IN WISCONSIN

Sagard,[1] whose work was published in 1636, tells us that the Hurons, who traded with the French, visited the Winnebagoes and the Fire Nation (Mascoutins),[2] bartering goods

1 Histoire du Canada, pp. 193–94 (Edition of 1866).
2 Dablon, Jesuit Relations, 1671.

for peltries. Champlain, the famous fur-trader, who represented the Company of the Hundred Associates,[3] formed by
Richelieu to monopolize the fur trade of New France and
govern the country, sent an agent named Jean Nicolet, in
1634,[4] to Green bay and Fox river to make a peace between
the Hurons and the Winnebagoes in the interests of inter-
tribal commerce. The importance of this phase of the trade
as late as 1681 may be inferred from these words of Du
Chesneau, speaking of the Ottawas, and including under
the term the Petun Hurons and the Chippeways also:
"Through them we obtain beaver, and although they, for
the most part, do not hunt, and have but a small portion
of peltry in their country, they go in search of it to the most
distant places, and exchange for it our merchandise which
they procure at Montreal." Among the tribes enumerated
as dealing with the Ottawas are the Sioux, Sauks, Pottawattomies, Winnebagoes, Menomonees and Mascoutins—all
Wisconsin Indians at this time. He adds: "Some of these
tribes occasionally come down to Montreal, but usually they
do not do so in very great numbers because they are too far
distant, are not expert at managing canoes, and because the
other Indians intimidate them, in order to be the carriers
of their merchandise and to profit thereby."[5]

It was the aim of the authorities to attract the Indians to
Montreal, or to develop the inter-tribal communication, and
thus to centralize the trade and prevent the dissipation of
the energies of the colony; but the temptations of the free

---

[3] See Parkman, Pioneers, p. 429ff. (1890).

[4] Margry, I., p. 50. The date rests on inference; see Bibliography of Nicolet
in Wis. Hist. Colls., XI., and cf. Hebberd, Wisconsin under French Dominion, p. 14.

[5] N. Y. Col. Docs., IX., p. 160.

forest traffic were too strong. In a memoir of 1697, Aubert de la Chesnaye says:

"At first the French went only among the Hurons, and since then to Missilimakinak, where they sold their goods to the savages of the places, who in turn went to exchange them with other savages in the depths of the woods, lands and rivers. But at present the French, having licenses, in order to secure greater profit surreptitiously, pass all the Ottawas and savages of Missilimakinak in order to go themselves to seek the most distant tribes, which is very displeasing to the former. *It is they, also, who have made excellent discoveries*; and four or five hundred young men, the best men of Canada, are engaged in this business. . . . They have given us knowledge of many names of savages that we did not know; and four or five hundred leagues more remote are others who are unknown to us."[6]

Two of the most noteworthy of these *coureurs de bois*, or wood-rangers, were Radisson and Groseilliers.[7] In 1660 they returned to Montreal with 300 Algonquins and sixty canoes laden with furs, after a voyage in which they visited, among other tribes, the Pottawattomies, Mascoutins, Sioux, and Hurons, in Wisconsin. From the Hurons they learned of the Mississippi, and probably visited the river. They soon returned from Montreal to the northern Wisconsin region. In the course of their wanderings they had a post at Chequamegon bay, and they ascended the Pigeon river, thus opening the Grand Portage route to the heart of Canada. Among their exploits they induced England to enter the Hudson

6 Margry, VI., p. 3; Coll. de Manuscrits, I., p. 255, where the date is wrongly given as 1676. The italics are ours.

7 Radisson, Voyages (Prince Soc. Pubs.); Margry, I., pp. 53–55, 83; Jes. Rels., 1660; Wis. Hist. Colls., X., XI; Narrative and Critical Hist. Amer., IV., pp. 168–73.

Bay trade, and gave the impetus that led to the organization of the Hudson Bay Company. The reports which these traders brought back had a most important effect in fostering exploration in the Northwest, and led to the visit of Menard, who was succeeded by Allouez, the pioneers of the Jesuits in Wisconsin.[8] Radisson gives us a good account of the early Wisconsin trade. Of his visit to the Ottawas he says:

"We weare wellcomed & made of saying that we weare the Gods and devils of the earth; that we should fournish them, & that they would bring us to their enemy to destroy them. We tould them [we] were very well content. We persuaded them first to come peaceably, not to distroy them presently, and if they would not condescend then would wee throw away the hatchett and make use of our thunders. We sent ambassadors to them wth guifts. That nation called Pontonatemick[9] wthout more adoe comes and meets us with the rest, and peace was concluded." "The savages," he writes, "love knives better than we serve God, which should make us blush for shame." In another place, "We went away free from any burden whilst those poore miserable thought themselves happy to carry our Equipage for the hope that they had that we should give them a brasse ring, or an awle, or an needle."[10] We find them using this influence in various places to make peace between hostile tribes, whom they threatened with punishment. This early commerce was carried on under the fiction of an exchange of presents. For example, Radisson says: "We gave them severall gifts and received many. They bestowed upon us above 300 robs of

8 Cf. Radisson, pp. 173–75, and Jes. Rels., 1660, pp. 12, 30; 1663, pp. 17ff.
9 Pottawattomies in the region of Green Bay.
10 Wis. Hist. Colls., XI., pp. 67–68.

castors out of wch we brought not five to the ffrench being far in the country."[11] Among the articles used by Radisson in this trade were kettles, hatchets, knives, graters, awls, needles, tin lookingglasses, little bells, ivory combs, vermilion, sword blades, necklaces and bracelets. The sale of guns and blankets was at this time exceptional, nor does it appear that Radisson carried brandy in this voyage.[12]

More and more the young men of Canada continued to visit the savags at their villages. By 1660 the *coureurs de bois* formed a distinct class,[13] who, despite the laws against it, pushed from Michillimackinac into the wilderness. Wisconsin was a favorite resort for these adventurers. By the time of the arrival of the Jesuits they had made themselves entirely at home upon our lakes. They had preceded Allouez at Chequamegon bay, and when he established his mission at Green bay he came at the invitation of the Pottawattomies, who wished him to "mollify some young Frenchmen who were among them for the purpose of trading and who threatened and ill-treated them."[14] He found fur traders before him on the Fox and the Wolf. Bancroft's assertion[15] that "religious enthusiasm took possession of the wilderness on the upper lakes and explored the Mississippi," is misleading. It is not true that "not a cape was turned, nor a mission founded, nor a river entered, nor a setlement begun, but a Jesuit led the way." In fact the Jesuits followed the traders;[16]

11 *Ibid.* XI., p. 90.
12 Radisson, pp. 200, 217, 219.
13 Sulte, in Transactions of the Wisconsin Academy of Science, Arts and Letters, V., p. 141; N. Y. Col. Docs., IX., pp. 153, 140, 152; Margry, VI., p. 3; Parkman, Old Régime, pp. 310–15.
14 Cf. Jes. Rels., 1670, p. 92.
15 History of United States, II., p. 138 (1884).
16 Harrisse, Notes sur la Nouvelle France, pp. 174–81.

their missions were on the sites of trading posts, and they themselves often traded.[17]

When St. Lusson, with the *coureur de bois*, Nicholas Perrot, took official possession of the Northwest for France at the Sault Ste. Marie in 1671, the cost of the expedition was defrayed by trade in beaver.[18] Joliet, who, accompanied by Marquette, descended the Mississippi by the Fox and Wisconsin route in 1673, was an experienced fur trader. While Du Lhut, chief of the *coureurs de bois*, was trading on Lake Superior, La Salle,[19] the greatest of these merchants, was preparing his far-reaching scheme for colonizing the Indians in the Illinois region under the direction of the French, so that they might act as a check on the inroads of the Iroquois, and aid in his plan of securing an exit for the furs of the Northwest, particularly buffalo hides, by way of the Mississippi and the Gulf. La Salle's "Griffen," the earliest ship to sail the Great Lakes, was built for this trade, and received her only cargo at Green Bay. Accault, one of La Salle's traders, with Hennepin, met Du Lhut on the upper Mississippi, which he had reached by way of the Bois Brulé and St. Croix, in 1680. Du Lhut's trade awakened the jealousy of La Salle, who writes in 1682: "If they go by way of the Ouisconsing, where for the present the chase of the buffalo is carried on and where I have commenced an establishment, they will ruin the trade on which alone I rely, on account of the great number of buffalo which are taken there every year, almost beyond belief."[20] Speaking of the

17 Parkman, Old Régime, p. 328ff., and La Salle, p. 98; Margry, II., p. 251; Radisson, p. 173.

18 See Talon's report quoted in Narr. and Crit. Hist. Amer., IV, p. 175.

19 Margry abounds in evidences of La Salle's commercial activity, as does Parkman's La Salle. See also Dunn, Indiana, pp. 20–21.

20 Margry, II., p. 254.

Jesuits at Green Bay, he declares that they "have in truth the key to the beaver country, where a brother blacksmith that they have and two companions convert more iron into beaver than the fathers convert savages into Christians."[21] Perrot says that the beaver north of the mouth of the Wisconsin were better than those of the Illinois country, and the chase was carried on in this region for a longer period;[22] and we know from Dablon that the Wisconsin savages were not compelled to separate by families during the hunting season, as was common among other tribes, because the game here was so abundant.[23] Aside from its importance as a key to the Northwestern trade, Wisconsin seems to have been a rich field of traffic itself.

With such extensive operations as the foregoing in the region reached by Wisconsin rivers, it is obvious that the government could not keep the *coureurs de bois* from the woods. Even governors like Frontenac connived at the traffic and shared its profits. In 1681 the government decided to issue annual licenses,[24] and messengers were dispatched to announce amnesty to the *coureurs de bois* about Green Bay and the south shore of Lake Superior.[25]

We may now offer some conclusions upon the connection of the fur trade with French explorations:

1. The explorations were generally induced and almost always rendered profitable by the fur trade. In addition to what has been presented on this point, note the following:

In 1669, Patoulet writes to Colbert concerning La Salle's

21 Margry, II., p. 251.
22 Tailhan's Perrot, p. 57.
23 Jes. Rels., 1670.
24 La Hontan, I., p. 53; N. Y. Col. Docs., IX., p. 159; Parkman, Old Régime, p. 305.
25 Margry, VI., p. 45.

voyage to explore a passage to Japan: "The enterprise is difficult and dangerous, but the good thing about it is that the King will be at no expense for this pretended discovery."[26]

The king's instructions to Governor De la Barre in 1682 say that, "Several inhabitants of Canada, excited by the hope of the profit to be realized from the trade with the Indians for furs, have undertaken at various periods discoveries in the countries of the Nadoussioux, the river Mississipy, and other parts of America."[27]

2. The early traders were regarded as quasi-supernatural beings by the Indians.[28] They alone could supply the coveted iron implements, the trinkets that tickled the savage's fancy, the "fire-water," and the guns that gave such increased power over game and the enemy. In the course of a few years the Wisconsin savages passed from the use of the implements of the stone age to the use of such an important product of the iron age as firearms. They passed also from the economic stage in which their hunting was for food and clothing simply, to that stage in which their hunting was made systematic and stimulated by the European demand for furs. The trade tended to perpetuate the hunter stage by making it profitable, and it tended to reduce the Indian to economic dependence[29] upon the Europeans, for while he learned to use the white man's gun he did not learn to make it or even to mend it. In this transition stage from their primitive condition the influence of the trader over the Indians was

26 Margry, I., p. 81.
27 N. Y. Col. Docs., IX., p. 167. On the cost of such expeditions, see documents in Margry, I., pp. 293–96; VI., pp. 503–507. On the profits of the trade, see La Salle in 2 Penna. Archives, VI., pp. 18–19.
28 See Radisson, *ante*, p. 28.
29 *Vide post*, p. 70.

all-powerful. The pre-eminence of the individual Indian who owned a gun made all the warriors of the tribe eager to possess like power. The tribe thus armed placed their enemies at such a disadvantage that they too must have like weapons or lose their homes.[30] No wonder that La Salle was able to say: "The savages take better care of us French than of their own children. From us only can they get guns and goods."[31] This was the power that France used to support her in the struggle with England for the Northwest.

3. The trader used his influence to promote peace between the Northwestern Indians.[32]

2. French Posts in Wisconsin

In the governorship of Dongan of New York, as has been noted, the English were endeavoring to secure the trade of the Northwest. As early as 1685, English traders had reached Michillimackinac, the depot of supplies for the *coureur de bois*, where they were cordially received by the Indians, owing to their cheaper goods.[33] At the same time the English on Hudson Bay were drawing trade to their posts in that region. The French were thoroughly alarmed. They saw the necessity of holding the Indians by trading posts in their midst, lest they should go to the English, for as Begon declared, the savages "always take the part of those with whom they trade."[34] It is at this time that the French occupa-

[30] *Vide ante*, p. 14; Radisson, p. 154; Minn. Hist. Colls., V., p. 427. Compare the effects of the introduction of bronze weapons into Europe.

[31] Margry, II., p. 284. On the power possessed by the French through this trade consult also D'Iberville's plan for locating Wisconsin Indians on the Illinois by changing their trading posts; see Margry, IV., pp. 586–98.

[32] Wis., Hist. Colls., XI., pp. 67–68, 90; Narr. and Crit. Hist. Amer., IV., p. 182; Perrot, p. 327; Margry, VI., pp. 507–509, 653–54.

[33] N. Y. Col. Docs., IX., pp. 296, 308; IV., p. 735.

[34] Quoted in Sheldon, Early History of Michigan, p. 310.

tion of the Northwest begins to assume a new phase. Stockaded trading posts were established at such key-points as a strait, a portage, a river-mouth, or an important lake, where also were Indian villages. In 1685 the celebrated Nicholas Perrot was given command of Green Bay and its dependencies.[35] He had trading posts near Trempealeau and at Fort St. Antoine on the Wisconsin side of Lake Pepin where he traded with the Sioux, and for a time he had a post and worked the lead-mines above the Des Moines river. Both these and Fort St. Nicholas at the mouth of the Wisconsin[36] were dependencies of Green Bay. Du Lhut probably established Fort St. Croix at the portage between the Bois Brulé river and the St. Croix.[37] In 1695 Le Sueur built a fort on the largest island above Lake Pepin, and he also asked the command of the post of Chequamegon.[38]

These official posts were supported by the profits of Indian commerce,[39] and were designed to keep the northwestern tribes at peace, and to prevent the English and Iroquois influence from getting the fur trade.

3. THE FOX WARS

In 1683 Perrot had collected Wisconsin Indians for an attack on the Iroquois, and again in 1686 he led them

[35] Tailhan's Perrot, p. 156.
[36] Wis. Hist. Colls., X., pp. 54, 300–302, 307, 321.
[37] Narr. and Crit. Hist. Amer., IV., p. 186.
[38] Margry, VI., p. 60. Near Ashland, Wis.
[39] Consult French MSS., 3d series, VI., Parl. Library, Ottawa, cited in Minn. Hist. Colls., V., p. 422; Id., V., p. 425. In 1731 M. La Ronde, having constructed at his own expense a bark of forty tons on Lake Superior, received the post of La Pointe de Chagouamigon as a gratuity to defray his expenses. See also the story of Verenderye's posts, in Parkman's article in *Atlantic Monthly*, June, 1887, and Margry, VI. See also 2 Penna. Archives, VI., p. 18; La Hontan, I., p. 53; N. Y. Col. Docs., IX., p. 159; Tailhan, Perrot, p. 302.

against the same enemy. But the efforts of the Iroquois and
the English to enter the region with their cheaper and better
goods, and the natural tendency of savages to plunder when
assured of supplies from other sources, now overcame the
control which the French had exercised. The Sauks and
Foxes, the Mascoutins, Kickapoos and Miamis, as has been
described, held the Fox and Wisconsin route to the West,
the natural and easy highway to the Mississippi, as La Hontan calls it.[40] Green Bay commanded this route, as La Pointe
de Chagouamigon[41] commanded the Lake Superior route
to the Bois Brulé and the St. Croix. One of Perrot's main
objects was to supply the Sioux on the other side of the
Mississippi, and these were the routes to them. To the
Illinois region, also, the Fox route was the natural one.
The Indians of this waterway therefore held the key to the
French position, and might attempt to prevent the passage
of French goods and support English influence and trade,
or they might try to monopolize the intermediate trade
themselves, or they might try to combine both policies.

As early as 1687 the Foxes, Mascoutins and Kickapoos,
animated apparently by hostility to the trade carried on by
Perrot with the Sioux, their enemy at that time, threatened
to pillage the post at Green Bay.[42] The closing of the
Ottawa to the northern fur trade by the Iroquois for three
years, a blow which nearly ruined Canada in the days of
Frontenac, as Parkman has described,[43] not only kept vast
stores of furs from coming down from Michillimackinac; it
must, also, have kept goods from reaching the northwestern
Indians. In 1692 the Mascoutins, who attributed the death

40 La Hontan, I., p. 105.
41 Near Ashland, Wis.
42 Tailhan, Perrot, pp. 139, 302.
43 Frontenac, pp. 315–16. Cf. Perrot, p. 302.

of some of their men to Perrot, plundered his goods, and the Foxes soon entered into negotiation with the Iroquois.[44] Frontenac expressed great apprehension lest with their allies on the Fox and Wisconsin route they should remove eastward and come into connection with the Iroquois and the English, a grave danger to New France.[45] Nor was this apprehension without reason.[46] Even such docile allies as the Ottawas and Pottawattomies threatened to leave the French if goods were not sent to them wherewith to oppose their enemies. "They have powder and iron," complained an Ottawa deputy; "how can we sustain ourselves? Have compassion, then, on us, and consider that it is no easy matter to kill men with clubs."[47] By the end of the seventeenth century the disaffected Indians closed the Fox and Wisconsin route against French trade.[48] In 1699 an order was issued recalling the French from the Northwest, it being the design to concentrate French power at the nearer posts.[49] Detroit was founded in 1701 as a place to which to attract the northwestern trade and intercept the English. In 1702 the priest at St. Joseph reported that the English were sending presents to the Miamis about that post and desiring to form an establishment in their country.[50] At the same date we find D'Iberville, of Louisiana, proposing a scheme for drawing the Miamis, Mascoutins andKickapoos from the Wisconsin streams to the Illinois, by changing their trading posts from Green Bay to the latter region, and drawing the

44 Perrot, p. 331; N. Y. Col. Docs., IX., 633.
45 *Ibid.*
46 N. Y. Col. Docs., IV., pp. 732–37.
47 N. Y. Col. Docs., IX., p. 673.
48 Shea, Early Voyages, p. 49.
49 Kingsford, Canada, II., p. 394; N. Y. Col. Docs., IX., p. 635.
50 Margry, V., p. 219.

Illinois by trading posts to the lower Ohio.[51] It was shortly after this that the Miamis and Kickapoos passed south under either the French or English influence,[52] and the hostility of the Foxes became more pronounced. A part of the scheme of La Motte Cadillac at Detroit was to colonize Indians about that post,[53] and in 1712 Foxes, Sauks, Mascoutins, Kickapoos, Pottawattomies, Hurons, Ottawas, Illinois, Menomonees and others were gathered there under the influence of trade. But soon, whether by design of the French and their allies or otherwise, hostilities broke out against the Foxes and their allies. The animus of the combat appears in the cries of the Foxes as they raised red blankets for flags and shouted "We have no father but the English!" while the allies of the French replied, "The English are cowards; they destroy the Indians with brandy and are enemies of the true God!" The Foxes were defeated with great slaughter and driven back to Wisconsin.[54] From this time until 1734 the French waged war against the Foxes with but short intermissions. The Foxes allied themselves with the Iroquois and the Sioux, and acted as middlemen between the latter and the traders, refusing passage to goods on the ground that it would damage their own trade to allow this.[55] They fostered hostilities between their old foes the Chippeways and their new allies the Sioux, and thus they cut off English intercourse with the latter by way of the north. This trade between the Chippeways and the Sioux was important to the French, and commandants were repeatedly sent to La Pointe

51 *Ibid.*, IV., p. 597.
52 Wis. Hist. Colls., III., p. 149; Smith, Wisconsin, II., p. 315.
53 Coll. de Manus., III., p. 622.
54 See Hebberd's account, Wisconsin under French Dominion; Coll. de Manus., I., p. 623; Smith, Wisconsin, II., p. 315.
55 Margry, VI., p. 543.

de Chagouamigon and the upper Mississippi to make peace between the two tribes.[56] While the wars were in progress the English took pains to enforce their laws against furnishing Indian goods to French traders. The English had for a time permitted this, and their own Indian trade had suffered because the French were able to make use of the cheap English goods. By their change in policy the English now brought home to the savages the fact that French goods were dearer.[57] Moreover, English traders were sent to Niagara to deal directly with "the far Indians," and the Foxes visited the English and Iroquois, and secured a promise that they might take up their abode with the latter and form an additional member of the confederacy in case of need.[58] As a counter policy the French attempted to exterminate the Foxes, and detached the Sioux from their alliance with the Foxes by establishing Fort Beauharnois, a trading post on the Minnesota side of Lake Pepin.[59]

The results of these wars were as follows:

1. They spread the feeling of defection among the North-western Indians, who could no longer be restrained, as at first, by the threat of cutting off their trade, there being now rivals in the shape of the English, and the French traders from Louisiana.[60]

2. They caused a readjustment of the Indian map of Wisconsin. The Mascoutins and the Pottawattomies had

[56] Tailhan, Perrot, *passim*; N. Y. Col. Docs., IX., pp. 570, 619, 621; Margry, VI., pp. 507–509, 553, 653–54; Minn. Hist. Colls., V., pp. 422, 425; Wis. Hist. Colls., III., p. 154.

[57] N. Y. Col. Docs., V., p. 726ff.

[58] *Ibid.*, IV., pp. 732, 735, 796–97; V., 687, 911.

[59] Margry, VI., pp. 553, 563, 575–80; Neill in *Mag. Western History*, November, 1887.

[60] Perrot, p. 148; Parkman, Montcalm and Wolfe, I., p. 42; Hebberd, Wisconsin under French Dominion, chapters on the Fox wars.

already moved southward to the Illinois country. Now the Foxes, driven from their river, passed first to Prairie du Chien and then down the Mississippi. The Sauks went at first to the Wisconsin, near Sauk Prairie, and then joined the Foxes. The Winnebagoes gradually extended themselves along the Fox and Wisconsin. The Chippeways,[61] freed from their fear of the Foxes, to whom the Wolf and the Wisconsin had given access to the northern portion of the state, now passed south to Lac du Flambeau,[62] to the headwaters of the Wisconsin, and to Lac Court Oreilles.[63]

3. The closing of the Fox and Wisconsin route fostered that movement of trade and exploration which at this time began to turn to the far Northwest along the Pigeon river route into central British America, in search of the Sea of the West,[64] whereby the Rocky Mountains were discovered; and it may have aided in turning settlement into the Illinois country.

4. These wars were a part of a connected series, including the Iroquois wars, the Fox wars, the attack of the Wisconsin trader, Charles de Langlade, upon the center of English trade at Pickawillany,[65] Ohio, and the French and Indian war that followed. All were successive stages of the struggle against English trade in the French possessions.

4. FRENCH SETTLEMENT IN WISCONSIN

Settlement was not the object of the French in the Northwest. The authorities saw as clearly as do we that the field was too vast for the resources of the colony, and they desired

61 Minn. Hist. Colls., V., pp. 190–91.
62 Oneida county.
63 Sawyer county.
64 Margry, VI.
65 Parkman, Montcalm and Wolfe, I., p. 84, and citations; *vide post*, p. 46.

to hold the region as a source of peltries, and contract their settlements. The only towns worthy of the name in the Northwest were Detroit and the settlements in Indiana and Illinois, all of which depended largely on the fur trade.[66] But in spite of the government the traffic also produced the beginnings of settlement in Wisconsin. About the middle of the century, Augustin de Langlade had made Green Bay his trading post. After Pontiac's war,[67] Charles de Langlade[68] made the place his permanent residence, and a little settlement grew up. At Prairie du Chien French traders annually met the Indians, and at this time there may have been a stockaded trading post there, but it was not a permanent settlement until the close of the Revolutionary war. Chequamegon bay was deserted[69] at the outbreak of the French war. There may have been a regular trading post at Milwaukee in this period, but the first trader recorded is not until 1762.[70] Doubtless wintering posts existed at other points in Wisconsin.

The characteristic feature of French occupancy of the Northwest was the trading post, and an illustration of it, and of the centralized administration of the French, the following account of De Repentigny's fort at Sault Ste. Marie (Michigan) is given in the words of Governor La Jonquière to the minister for the colonies in 1751:[71]

"He arrived too late last year at the Sault Ste. Marie to fortify himself well; however, he secured himself in a sort of

[66] Fergus, Historical Series, No. 12; Breese, Early History of Illinois; Dunn, Indiana; Hubbard, Memorials of a Half Century; Monette, History of the Valley of the Mississippi, I., ch. iv.

[67] Henry Travels, ch. x.

[68] See Memoir in Wis. Hist. Colls., VII.; III., p. 224; VII., pp. 127, 152, 166.

[69] Henry, Travels.

[70] Wis. Hist. Colls., I., p. 35.

[71] Minn. Hist. Colls., V., pp. 435–36.

fort large enough to receive the traders of Missilimakinac
. . . . He employed his hired men during the whole winter
in cutting 1100 pickets of fifteen feet for his fort, with the
doublings, and the timber necessary for the construction of
three houses, one of them thirty feet long by twenty wide,
and two others twenty-five feet long and the same width as
the first. His fort is entirely furnished with the exception of
a redoubt of oak, which he is to have made twelve feet
square, and which shall reach the same distance above the
gate of the fort. His fort is 110 feet square.

"As for the cultivation of the lands, the Sieur de Repentigny has a bull, two bullocks, three cows, two heifers, one
horse and a mare from Missilimakinac . . . . He has engaged
a Frenchman who married at Sault Ste. Marie an Indian
woman to take a farm; they have cleared it and sowed it, and
without a frost they will gather 30 to 35 sacks of corn. The
said Sieur de Repentigny so much feels it his duty to devote
himself to the cultivation of these lands that he has already
entered into a bargain for two slaves[72] whom he will employ
to take care of the corn[73] that he will gather upon these
lands."

5. The Traders' Struggle to Retain their Trade

While they had been securing the trade of the far Northwest and the Illinois country, the French had allowed the

[72] Indians. Compare Wis. Hist. Colls., III., p. 256; VII., pp. 158, 117, 179.

[73] The French minister for the colonies expressing approval of this post,
writes in 1752: "As it can hardly be expected that any other grain than
corn will grow there, it is necessary at least for a while to stick to it, and
not to persevere stubbornly in trying to raise wheat." On this Dr. E. D.
Neill comments: "Millions of bushels of wheat from the region west and
north of Lake Superior pass every year . . . through the ship canal at Sault
Ste. Marie." The corn was for supplying the voyageurs.

English to gain the trade of the upper Ohio,[74] and were now brought face to face with the danger of losing the entire Northwest, and thus the connection of Canada and Louisiana. The commandants of the western posts were financially as well as patriotically interested. In 1754, Green Bay, then garrisoned by an officer, a sergeant and four soldiers, required for the Indian trade of its department thirteen canoes of goods annually, costing about 7000 livres each, making a total of nearly $18,000.[75] Bougainville asserts that Marin, the commandant of the department of the Bay, was associated in trade with the governor and intendant, and that his part netted him annually 15,000 francs.

When it became necessary for the French to open hostilities with the English traders in the Ohio country, it was the Wisconsin trader, Charles de Langlade, with his Chippeway Indians, who in 1752 fell upon the English trading post at Pickawillany and destroyed the center of English trade in the Ohio region.[76] The leaders in the opening of the war that ensued were Northwestern traders. St. Pierre, who commanded at Fort Le Bœuf when Washington appeared with his demands from the Governor of Virginia that the French should evacuate the Ohio country, had formerly been the trader in command at Lake Pepin on the upper Mississippi.[77] Coulon de Villiers, who captured Washington at Fort Necessity, was the son of the former commandant at Green Bay.[78] Beaujeu, who led the French troops to the

[74] Margry, VI., p. 758.
[75] Canadian Archives, 1886, clxxii.
[76] Parkman, Montcalm and Wolfe, I., p. 84.
[77] Minn. Hist. Colls., V., p. 433. Washington was guided to the fort along an old trading route by traders; the trail was improved by the Ohio Company, and was used by Braddock in his march (Sparks, Washington's Works, II., p. 302).
[78] Wis. Hist. Colls., V., p. 117.

defeat of Braddock, had been an officer in the Fox wars.[79] It was Charles de Langlade who commanded the Indians and was chiefly responsible for the success of the ambuscade.[80] Wisconsin Indians, representing almost all the tribes, took part with the French in the war.[81] Traders passed to and from their business to the battlefields of the East. For example, De Repentigny, whose post at Sault Ste. Marie has been described, was at Michillimackinac in January, 1755, took part in the battle of Lake George in the fall of that year, formed a partnership to continue the trade with a trader of Michillimackinac in 1756, was at that place in 1758, and in 1759 fought with Montcalm on the heights of Abraham.[82] It was not without a struggle that the traders yielded their beaver country.

6. THE ENGLISH AND THE NORTHWEST: INFLUENCE OF THE INDIAN TRADE ON DIPLOMACY

In the meantime what was the attitude of the English toward the Northwest? In 1720 Governor Spotswood of Virginia wrote:[83] "The danger which threatens these, his Maj'ty's Plantations, from this new Settlement is also very considerable, for by the communication which the French may maintain between Canada and Mississippi by the conveniency of the Lakes, they do in a manner surround all the British Plantations. They have it in their power by these

---

[79] *Ibid.*, p. 115.

[80] Parkman, Montcalm and Wolfe, II., pp. 425–26. He was prominently engaged in other battles; see Wis. Hist. Colls., VII., pp. 123–87.

[81] Wis. Hist. Colls., V., p. 117.

[82] Neill, in *Mag. West. Hist.* VII., p. 17, and Minn. Hist. Colls., V., pp. 434–36. For other examples see Wis. Hist. Colls., V., pp. 113–18; Minn. Hist. Colls., V., pp. 430–31.

[83] Va. Hist. Colls., N. S., II., p. 329.

Lakes and the many Rivers running into them and into the Mississippi to engross all the Trade of the Indian Nations w'ch are now supplied from hence."

Cadwallader Colden, Surveyor-General of New York, says in 1724: "New France (as the French now claim) extends from the mouth of the Mississippi to the mouth of the River St. Lawrence, by which the French plainly shew their intention of enclosing the British Settlements and cutting us off from all Commerce with the numerous Nations of Indians that are everywhere settled over the vast continent of North America."[84] As time passed, as population increased, and as the reports of the traders extolled the fertility of the country, both the English and the French, but particularly the Americans, began to consider it from the standpoint of colonization as well as from that of the fur trade.[85] The Ohio Company had both settlement and the fur trade in mind,[86] and the French Governor, Galissonière, at the same period urged that France ought to plant a colony in the Ohio region.[87] After the conquest of New France by England there was still the question whether she should keep Canada and the Northwest.[88] Franklin, urging her to do so, offered as one argument the value of the fur trade, intrinsically and as a means of holding the Indians in check. Discussing the question whether the interior regions of America would ever be accessible to English settlement and so to English manufactures, he pointed out the vastness of our river and

84 N. Y. Col. Docs., V., p. 726.

85 Indian relations had a noteworthy influence upon colonial union; see Lucas, Appendiculae Historicae, p. 161, and Frothingham, Rise of the Republic, ch. iv.

86 Parkman, Montcalm and Wolfe, I., p. 59; Sparks, Washington's Works, II., p. 302.

87 Parkman, Montcalm and Wolfe, I., p., 21.

88 Ibid. II., p. 403.

lake system, and the fact that Indian trade already permeated the interior. In interesting comparison he called their attention to the fact that English commerce reached along river systems into the remote parts of Europe, and that in ancient times the Levant had carried on a trade with the distant interior.[89]

That the value of the fur trade was an important element in inducing the English to retain Canada is shown by the fact that Great Britain no sooner came into the possession of the country than she availed herself of the fields for which she had so long intrigued. Among the western posts she occupied Green Bay, and with the garrison came traders;[90] but the fort was abandoned on the outbreak of Pontiac's war.[91] This war was due to the revolt of the Indians of the Northwest against the transfer of authority, and was fostered by the French traders.[92] It concerned Wisconsin but slightly, and at its close we find Green Bay a little trading community along the Fox, where a few families lived comfortably[93] under the quasi-patriarchal rule of Langlade.[94] In 1765 trade was re-established at Chequamegon Bay by an English trader named Henry, and here he found the Chippeways dressed in deerskins, the wars having deprived them of a trader.[95]

As early as 1766 some Scotch merchants more extensively reopened the fur trade, using Michillimackinac as the basis

[89] Bigelow, Franklin's Works, III., pp. 43, 83, 98–100.

[90] Wis. Hist. Colls., I., pp. 26–38.

[91] Parkman, Pontiac, I., 185. Consult N. Y. Col. Docs., VI., pp. 635, 690, 788, 872, 974.

[92] Wis. Hist. Colls., I., p. 26.

[93] Carver, Travels.

[94] Porlier Papers, Wis. Fur Trade MSS., in possession of Wis. Hist. Soc.; also Wis. Hist. Colls., III., pp. 200–201.

[95] Henry, Travels.

of their operations and employing French voyageurs.[96] By the proclamation of the King in 1763 the Northwest was left without political organization, it being reserved as crown lands and exempt from purchase or settlement, the design being to give up to the Indian trade all the lands "westward of the sources of the rivers which fall into the sea from the West and Northwest as aforesaid." In a report of the Lords Commissioners for Trade and Plantations in 1772 we find the attitude of the English government clearly set forth in these words:[97]

"The great object of colonization upon the continent of North America has been to improve and extend the commerce and manufactures of this kingdom . . . It does appear to us that the extension of the fur trade depends entirely upon the Indians being undisturbed in the possession of their hunting grounds, and that all colonization does in its nature and must in its consequence operate to the prejudice of that branch of commerce . . . Let the savages enjoy their deserts in quiet. Were they driven from their forests the peltry trade would decrease."

In a word, the English government attempted to adopt the western policy of the French. From one point of view it was a successful policy. The French traders took service under the English, and in the Revolutionary war Charles de Langlade led the Wisconsin Indians to the aid of Hamilton against George Rogers Clark,[98] as he had before against the British, and in the War of 1812 the British trader Robert Dickson repeated this movement.[99] As in the days of Begon,

96 Canadian Archives, 1888, p. 61 ff.
97 Sparks, Franklin's Works, IV., pp. 303–23.
98 Wis. Hist. Colls., XI.
99 *Ibid.*

"the savages took the part of those with whom they traded."
The secret proposition of Vergennes, in the negotiations
preceding the treaty of 1783, to limit the United States by
the Alleghanies and to give the Northwest to England, while
reserving the rest of the region between the mountains and
the Mississippi as Indian territory under Spanish protection,[100] would have given the fur trade to these nations.[101] In
the extensive discussions over the diplomacy whereby the
Northwest was included within the limits of the United
States, it has been asserted that we won our case by the
chartered claims of the colonies and by George Rogers
Clark's conquest of the Illinois country. It appears, however,
that in fact Franklin, who had been a prominent member
and champion of the Ohio Company, and who knew the
West from personal acquaintance, had persuaded Shelburne
to cede it to us as a part of a liberal peace that should
effect a reconciliation between the two countries. Shelburne
himself looked upon the region from the point of view of
the fur trade simply, and was more willing to make this
concession than he was some others. In the discussion over
the treaty in Parliament in 1783, the Northwestern boundary was treated almost solely from the point of view of the
fur trade and of the desertion of the Indians. The question
was one of profit and loss in this traffic. One member at-
tacked Shelburne on the ground that, "not thinking the
naked independence a sufficient proof of his liberality to the
United States, he had clothed it with the warm covering of
our fur trade." Shelburne defended his cession "on the fair

[100] Jay, Address before the N. Y. Hist. Soc. on the Treaty Negotiations of
1782–83, appendix; map in Narr. and Crit. Hist. Amer., VII., p. 148.

[101] But Vergennes had a just appreciation of the value of the region for
settlement as well. He recognized and feared the American capacity for
expansion.

rule of the value of the district ceded,"[102] and comparing exports and imports and the cost of administration, he concluded that the fur trade of the Northwest was not of sufficient value to warrant continuing the war. The most valuable trade, he argued, was north of the line, and the treaty merely applied sound economic principles and gave America "a share in the trade." The retention of her Northwestern posts by Great Britain at the close of the war, in contravention of the treaty, has an obvious relation to the fur trade. In his negotiations with Hammond, the British ambassador in 1791, Secretary of State Jefferson said: "By these proceedings we have been intercepted entirely from the commerce of furs with the Indian nations to the northward —a commerce which had ever been of great importance to the United States, not only for its intrinsic value, but as it was the means of cherishing peace with these Indians, and of superseding the necessity of that expensive warfare which we have been obliged to carry on with them during the time that these posts have been in other hands."[103]

In discussing the evacuation of the posts in 1794 Jay was met by a demand that complete freedom of the Northwestern Indian trade should be granted to British subjects. It was furthermore proposed by Lord Grenville[104] that, "Whereas it is now understood that the river Mississippi would at no point thereof be intersected by such westward line as is described in the said treaty [1783]; and whereas it was stipulated in the said treaty that the navigation of the Mississippi should be free to both parties"—one of two new

---

102 Hansard, XXIII., pp. 377–78, 381–83, 389, 398–99, 405, 409–10, 423, 450, 457, 465.

103 Amercian State Papers, Foreign Relations, I., p. 190.

104 *Ibid.*, p. 487.

propositions should be accepted regarding the northwestern boundary. The maps in American State Papers, Foreign Relations, I., 492, show that both these proposals extended Great Britain's territory so as to embrace the Grand Portage and the lake region of northern Minnesota, one of the best of the Northwest Company's fur-trading regions south of the line, and in connection by the Red river with the Canadian river systems.[105] They were rejected by Jay. Secretary Randolph urged him to hasten the removal of the British, stating that the delay asked for, to allow the traders to collect their Indian debts, etc., would have a bad effect upon the Indians, and protesting that free communication for the British would strike deep into our Indian trade.[106] The definitive treaty included the following provisions:[107] The posts were to be evacuated before June 1, 1796. "All settlers and traders, within the precincts or jurisdiction of the said posts, shall continue to enjoy, unmolested, all their property of every kind, and shall be protected therein. They shall be at full liberty to remain there, or to remove with all or any part of their effects; and it shall also be free to them to sell their lands, houses, or effects, or to retain the property thereof, at their discretion; such of them as shall continue to reside within the said boundary lines shall not be compelled to become citizens of the United States, or to take any oath

[105] As early as 1794 the company had established a stockaded fort at Sandy lake. After Jay's treaty conceding freedom of entry, the company dotted this region with posts and raised the British flag over them. In 1805 the center of trade was changed from Grand Portage to Fort William Henry, on the Canada side. Neill, Minnesota, p. 239 (4th edn.). Bancroft, Northwest Coast, I., p. 560. Vide ante, p. 21–22, and post, p. 62.

[106] Amer. State Papers, For. Rels., I., p. 509.

[107] Treaties and Conventions, etc., 1776–1887, p. 380.

of allegiance to the government thereof; but they shall be at full liberty to do so if they think proper, and they shall make and declare their election within one year after the evacuation aforesaid. And all persons who shall continue there after the expiration of the said year without having declared their intention of remaining subjects of his British Majesty shall be considered as having elected to become citizens of the United States." "It is agreed that it shall at all times be free of His Majesty's subjects, and to the Indians dwelling on either side of the said boundary line, freely to pass and repass by land or inland navigation into the respective territories and countries of the parties on the continent of America (the country within the limits of the Hudson's Bay Company only excepted), and to navigate all the lakes, rivers and waters thereof, and freely to carry on trade and commerce with each other."

In his elaboate defence of Jay's treaty, Alexander Hamilton paid much attention to the question of the fur trade. Defending Jay for permitting so long a delay in evacuation and for granting right of enry into our fields, he minimized the value of the trade. So far from being worth $800,000 annually, he asserted the trade within our limits would not be worth $100,000, seven-eighths of the traffic being north of the line. This estimate of the value of the northwestern trade was too low. In the course of his paper he made this observation:[108]

"In proportion as the article is viewed on an enlarged plan and permanent scale, its importance to us magnifies. Who can say how far Brtish colonization may spread southward and down the west side of the Mississippi, northward and westward into the vast interior regions towards the

[108] Lodge, Hamilton's Works, IV., p. 514.

Pacific ocean? . . . In this large view of the subject, the fur trade, which has made a very prominent figure in the discussion, becomes a point scarcely visible. Objects of great variety and magnitude start up in perspective, eclipsing the little atoms of the day, and promising to grow and mature with time."

Such was not the attitude of Great Britain. To her the Northwest was desirable on account of its Indian commerce. By a statement of the Province of Upper Canada, sent with the approbation of Lieutenant-General Hunter to the Duke of Kent, Commander-in-Chief of British North America, in the year 1800, we are enabled to see the situation through Canadian eyes:[109]

"The Indians, who had loudly and Justly complained of a treaty [1783] in which they were sacrificed by a cession of their country contrary to repeated promises, were with difficulty appeased, however finding the Posts retained and some Assurances given they ceased to murmur and resolved to defend their country extending from the Ohio Northward to the Great Lakes and westward to the Mississippi, an immense tract, in which they found the deer, the bear, the wild wolf, game of all sorts in profusion. They employed the Tomahawk and Scalping Knife against such deluded settlers who on the faith of the treaty to which they did not consent, ventured to cross the Ohio, secretly encouraged by the Agents of Government, supplied with Arms, Ammunition, and provisions they maintained an obstinate & destructive war against the States, cut off two Corps sent against them. . . . The American Government, discouraged by these disasters were desirous of peace on any terms, their deputies were sent to Detroit, they offered to confine their

109 Michigan Pioneer Colls., XV., p. 8; cf. pp. 10, 12, 23, and XVI., p. 67.

Pretensions within certain limits far South of the Lakes. If this offer had been accepted the Indian Country would have been for ages an impassible Barrier between us. twas unfortunately perhaps wantonly rejected, and the war continued."

Acting under the privileges accorded to them by Jay's treaty, the British traders were in almost as complete possession of Wisconsin until after the war of 1812 as if Great Britain still owned it. When the war broke out the keys of the region, Detroit and Michillimackinac, fell into the British hands. Green Bay and Prairie du Chien were settlements of French-British traders and voyageurs. Their leader was Robert Dickson, who had traded at the latter settlement. Writing in 1814 from his camp at Winnebago Lake, he says: "I think that Bony [Bonaparte] must be knocked up as all Europe are now in Arms. The crisis is not far off when I trust in God that the Tyrant will be humbled, & the Scoundrel American Democrats be obliged to go down on their knees to Britain."[110] Under him most of the Wisconsin traders of importance received British commissions. In the spring of 1814 the Americans took Prairie du Chien, at the mouth of the Wisconsin river, whereupon Col. M'Douall, the British commandant at Michillimackinac, wrote to General Drummond:[111] . . . "I saw at once the imperious necessity which existed of endeavoring by every means to dislodge the American Genl from his new conquest, and make him relinquish the immense tract of country he had seized upon in consequence & which brought him into the very heart of that occupied by our friendly Indians, There was no alterna-

---

110 Wis. Fur Trade MSS., 1814 (State Hist. Soc.).
111 Wis. Hist. Colls., XI., p. 260. Mich. Pioneer Colls., XVI., pp. 103–104.

tive it must either be done or there was an end to our connection with the Indians for if allowed to settle themselves by dint of threats bribes & sowing divisions among them, tribe after tribe would be gained over or subdued, & thus would be destroyed the only barrier which protects the great trading establishments of the North West and the Hudson's Bay Companys. Nothing could then prevent the enemy from gaining the source of the Mississippi, gradually extending themselves by the Red river to Lake Winnipic, from whense the descent of Nelsons river to York Fort would in time be easy."

The British traders, voyageurs and Indians[112] dislodged the Americans, and at the close of the war England was practically in possession of the Indian country of the Northwest.

In the negotiations at Ghent the British commissioners asserted the sovereignty of the Indians over their lands, and their independence in relation to the United States, and demanded that a barrier of Indian territory should be established between the two countries, free to the traffic of both nations but not open to purchase by either.[113] The line of the Grenville treaty was suggested as a basis for determining this Indian region. The proposition would have removed from the sovereignty of the United States the territory of the Northwest with the exception of about two-thirds of Ohio,[114] and given it over to the British fur traders. The Americans declined to grant the terms, and the United States was finally left in possession of the Northwest.

---

112 Wis. Hist. Colls., XI., p. 255. Cf. Mich. Pioneer Colls., XVI., p. 67. Rolette, one of the Prairie du Chien traders, was tried by the British for treason to Great Britain.

113 Amer. State Papers, For. Rels., III., p. 705.

114 Amer. State Papers, Ind. Affs., I., p. 562. See map in Collot's Travels, atlas.

7. The Northwest Company

The most striking feature of the English period was the Northwest Company.[115] From a study of it one may learn the character of the English occupation of the Northwest.[116] It was formed in 1783 and fully organized in 1787, with the design of contesting the field with the Hudson Bay Company. Goods were brought from England to Montreal, the headquarters of the company, and thence from the four emporiums, Detroit, Mackinaw, Sault Ste. Marie, and Grand Portage, they were scattered through the great Northwest, even to the Pacific ocean.

Toward the end of the eighteenth century ships[117] began to take part in this commerce; a portion of the goods was sent from Montreal in boats to Kingston, thence in vessels to Niagara, thence overland to Lake Erie, to be reshipped in vessels to Mackinaw and to Sault Ste. Marie, where another transfer was made to a Lake Superior vessel. These ships were of about ninety-five tons burden and made four or five trips a season. But in the year 1800 the primitive mode of trade was not materially changed. From the traffic along the main artery of commerce between Grand Portage and Montreal may be learned the kind of trade that flowed along such branches as that between the island of Mackinaw and

[115] On this company see Mackenzie, Voyages; Bancroft, Northwest Coast, I., 378–616, and citations; *Hunt's Merch. Mag.*, III., p. 185; Irving, Astoria; Ross, The Fur Hunters of the Far West; Harmon, Journal; Report on the Canadian Archives, 1881, p. 61 et seq. This fur-trading life still goes on in the more remote regions of British America. See Robinson, Great Fur Land, ch. xv.

[116] Wis. Hist. Colls., XI., pp. 123–25.

[117] Mackenzie, Voyages, p. xxxix. Harmon, Journal, p. 36. In the fall of 1784, Haldimand granted permission to the Northwest Company to build a small vessel at Detroit, to be employed next year on Lake Superior. Calendar of Canadian Archives, 1888, p. 72.

the Wisconsin posts. The visitor at La Chine rapids, near Montreal, might have seen a squadron of Northwestern trading canoes leaving for the Grand Portage, at the west of Lake Superior.[118]

The boatmen, or "engagés," having spent their season's gains in carousal, packed their blanket capotes and were ready for the wilderness again. They made a picturesque crew in their gaudy turbans, or hats adorned with plumes and tinsel, their brilliant handkerchiefs tied sailor-fashion about swarthy necks, their calico shirts, and their flaming worsted belts, which served to hold the knife and the tobacco pouch. Rough trousers, leggings, and cowhide shoes or gaily-worked moccasins completed the costume. The trading birch canoe measured forty feet in length, with a depth of three and a width of five. It floated four tons of freight, and yet could be carried by four men over difficult portages. Its crew of eight men was engaged at a salary[119] of from five to eight hundred livres, about $100 to $160 per annum, each, with a yearly outfit of coarse clothing and a daily food allowance of

[118] Besides the authorities cited above, see "Anderson's Narrative," in Wis. Hist. Colls., IX., pp. 137–206.

[119] An estimate of the cost of an expedition in 1717 is given in Margry, VI., p. 506. At that time the wages of a good voyageur for a year amounted to about $50. Provisions for the two months' trip from Montreal to Mackinaw cost about $1.00 per month per man. Indian corn for a year cost $16; lard, $10; *eau de vie*, $1.30; tobacco, 25 cents. It cost, therefore, less than $80 to support a voyageur for one year's trip into the woods. Gov. Ninian Edwards, writing at the time of the American Fur Company (*post*, p. 64), says: "The whole expense of transporting eight thousand weight of goods from Montreal to the Mississippi, wintering with the Indians, and returning with a load of furs and peltries in the succeeding season, including the cost of provisions and portages and the hire of five engagés for the whole time does not exceed five hundred and twenty-five dollars, much of which is usually paid to those engagés when in the Indian country, in goods at an exorbitant price." American State Papers, VI., p. 65.

a quart of hulled corn, or peas, seasoned with two ounces of tallow.

The experienced voyageurs who spent the winters in the woods were called *hivernans,* or winterers, or sometimes *hommes du nord*; while the inexperienced, those who simply made the trip from Montreal to the outlying depots and return, were contemptuously dubbed *mangeurs de lard*,[120] "pork-eaters," because their pampered appetites de-

---

[120] This distinction goes back at least to 1681 (N. Y. Col. Docs., IX., p. 152). Often the engagement was for five years, and the voyageur might be transferred from one master to another, at the master's will.

The following is a translation of a typical printed engagement, one of scores in the possession of the Wisconsin Historical Society, the written portions in brackets:

"Before a Notary residing at the post of Michilimakinac, Undersigned; Was Present [Joseph Lamarqueritte] who has voluntarily engaged and doth bind himself by these Presents to M[onsieur Louis Grignion] here present and accepting, at [his] first requisition to set off from this Post [in the capacity of Winterer] in one of [his] Canoes or Bateaux to make the Voyage [going as well as returning] and to winter for [two years at the Bay].

"And to have due and fitting care on the route and while at the said [place] of the Merchandise, Provisions, Peltries, Utensils and of everything necessary for the Voyage; to serve, obey and execute faithfully all that the said Sieur [Bourgeois] or any other person representing him to whom he may transport the present Engagement, commands him lawfully and honestly; to do [his] profit, to avoid anything to his damage, and to inform him of it if it come to his knowledge, and generally to do all that a good [Winterer] ought and is obliged to do; without power to make any particular trade, to absent himself, or to quit the said service, under pain of these Ordinances, and of loss of wages. This engagement is therefore made, for the sum of [Eight Hundred] livres or shillings, ancient currency of Quebec, that he promises [and] binds himself to deliver and pay to the said [Winterer one month] after his return to this Post, and at his departure [an Equipment each year of 2 Shirts, 1 Blanket of 3 point, 1 Carot of Tobacco, 1 Cloth Blanket, 1 Leather Shirt, 1 Pair of Leather Breeches, 5 Pairs of Leather Shoes, and Six Pounds of Soap.]

"For thus, etc., promising, etc., binding, etc., renouncing, etc.

"Done and passed at the said [Michilimackinac] in the year eighteen hundred [Seven] the [twenty-fourth] of [July before] twelve o'clock; & have signed with the exception of the said [Winterer] who, having declared

manded peas and pork rather than hulled corn and tallow. Two of the crew, one at the bow and the other at the stern, being especially skilled in the craft of handling the paddle in the rapids, received higher wages than the rest. Into the canoe was first placed the heavy freight, shot, axes, powder; next the dry goods, and, crowning all, filling the canoe to overflowing, came the provisions—pork, peas or corn, and sea biscuits, sewed in canvas sacks.

The lading completed, the voyageur hung his votive offerings in the chapel of Saint Anne, patron saint of voyageurs, the paddles struck the waters of the St. Lawrence, and the fleet of canoes glided away on its six weeks' journey to Grand Portage. There was the Ottawa to be ascended, the rapids to be run, the portages where the canoe must be emptied and where each voyageur must bear his two packs of ninety pounds apiece, and there were the *décharges*, where the canoe was merely lightened and where the voyageurs, now on the land, now into the rushing waters, dragged it forward till the rapids were passed. There was no stopping to dry, but on, until the time for the hasty meal, or the evening campfire underneath the pines. Every two miles there was a stop for a three minutes' smoke, or "pipe," and when a portage was made it was reckoned in "pauses," by which is meant the number of times the men must stop to rest. Whenever a burial cross appeared, or a stream was

himself unable to do so, has made his ordinary mark after the engagement was read to him.

his
"JOSEPH X LAMARQUERITTE. [SEAL]
mark.

"SAM^L. ABBOTT,   LOUIS GRIGNON. [SEAL]
   Not. Pub."
Endorsed—"Engagement of Joseph Lamarqueritte to Louis Grignon."

left or entered, the voyageurs removed their hats, and made
the sign of the cross while one of their number said a short
prayer; and again the paddles beat time to some rollicking
song.[121]

> Dans mon chemin, j'ai rencontré
> Trois cavalières, bien montées;
> L'on, lon, laridon daine,
> Lon, ton, laridon dai.
> Trois cavalières bien montées,
> L'un à cheval, et l'autre à pied;
> L'on, lon, laridon daine,
> Lon, ton, laridon dai.

Arrived at Sault Ste. Marie, the fleet was often doubled
by newcomers, so that sometimes sixty canoes swept their
way along the north shore, the paddles marking sixty strokes
a minute, while the rocks gave back the echoes of Canadian
songs rolling out from five hundred lusty throats. And so
they drew up at Grand Portage, near the present northeast
boundary of Minnesota, now a sleepy, squalid little village,
but then the general rendezvous where sometimes over a
thousand men met; for, at this time, the company had fifty
clerks, seventy interpreters, eighteen hundred and twenty
canoe-men, and thirty-five guides. It sent annually to Montreal 106,000 beaver-skins, to say nothing of other peltries.
When the proprietors from Montreal met the proprietors
from the northern posts, and with their clerks gathered at
the banquet in their large log hall to the number of a hundred, the walls hung with spoils of the chase, the rough
tables furnished with abundance of venison, fish, bread, salt

121 For Canadian boat-songs see *Hunt's Merch. Mag.*, III., p. 189; Mrs.
Kinzie, Wau Bun; Bela Hubbard, Memorials of a Half-Century; Robinson,
Great Fur Land.

pork, butter, peas, corn, potatoes, tea, milk, wine and *eau de vie*, while, outside, the motley crowd of engagés feasted on hulled corn and melted fat—was it not a truly baronial scene? Clerks and engagés of this company, or its rival, the Hudson Bay Company, might winter one season in Wisconsin and the next in the remote north. For example, Amable Grignon, a Green Bay trader, wintered in 1818 at Lac qui Parle in Minnesota, the next year at Lake Athabasca, and the third in the hyperborean regions of Great Slave Lake. In his engagement he figures as Amable Grignon, *of the Parish of Green Bay, Upper Canada*, and he receives $400 "and found in tobacco and shoes and two doges," besides "the usual equipment given to clerks." He afterwards returned to a post on the Wisconsin river. The attitude of Wisconsin traders toward the Canadian authorities and the Northwestern wilds is clearly shown in this document, which brings into a line Upper Canada, "the parish of Green Bay," and the Hudson Bay Company's territories about Great Slave Lake![122]

How widespread and how strong was the influence of these traders upon the savages may be easily imagined, and this commercial control was strengthened by the annual presents made to the Indians by the British at their posts. At a time when our relations with Great Britain were growing strained, such a power in the Northwest was a serious menace.[123] In 1809 John Jacob Astor secured a charter from

---

[122] Wis. Fur Trade MSS. (Wis. Hist. Soc.). Published in Proceedings of the Thirty-Sixth Annual Meeting of the State Hist. Soc. of Wis. 1889, pp. 81–82.

[123] See Mich. Pioneer Colls., XV., XVI., pp. 67, 74. The government consulted the Northwest Company, who made particular efforts to "prevent the Americans from ever alienating the minds of the Indians." To this end they drew up memoirs regarding the proper frontiers.

the State of New York, incorporating the American Fur Company. He proposed to consolidate the fur trade of the United States, plant an establishment in the contested Oregon territory, and link it with Michillimackinac (Mackinaw island) by way of the Missouri through a series of trading posts. In 1810 two expeditions of his Pacific Fur Company set out for the Columbia, the one around Cape Horn and the other by way of Green bay and the Missouri. In 1811 he bought a half interest in the Mackinaw Company, a rival of the Northwest Company and the one that had especial power in Wisconsin and Minnesota, and this new organization he called the Southwest Company. But the war of 1812 came; Astoria, the Pacific post, fell into the hands of the Northwest Company, while the Southwest Company's trade was ruined.

8. American Influences

Although the Green Bay court of justice, such as it was, had been administered under American commissions since 1803, when Reaume dispensed a rude equity under a commission of Justice of the Peace from Governor Harrison,[124] neither Green Bay nor the rest of Wisconsin had any proper appreciation of its American connections until the close of this war. But now occurred these significant events:

1. Astor's company was reorganized as the American Fur Company, with headquarters at Mackinaw island.[125]

2. The United States enacted in 1816 that neither foreign

[124] Reaume's petition in Wis. Fur Trade MSS. in possession of Wisconsin Historical Society.

[125] On this company consult Irving, Astoria; Bancroft, Northwest Coast, I., ch. xvi.; II., chs. vii–x; *Mag. Amer. Hist.* XIII., p. 269; Franchere, Narrative; Ross, Adventures of the First Settlers on the Oregon, or Columbia River (1849); Wis. Fur Trade MSS. (State Hist. Soc.).

fur traders, nor capital for that trade, should be admitted to this country.[126] This was designed to terminate English influence among the tribes, and it fostered Astor's company. The law was so interpreted as not to exclude British (that is generally, French) interpreters and boatmen, who were essential to the company; but this interpretation enabled British subjects to evade the law and trade on their own account by having their invoices made out to some Yankee clerk, while they accompanied the clerk in the guise of interpreters.[127] In this way a number of Yankees came to the State.

3. In the year 1816 United States garrisons were sent to Green Bay and Prairie du Chien.[128]

4. In 1814 the United States provided for locating government trading posts at these two places.

9. Government Trading Houses

The system of public trading houses goes back to colonial days. At first in Plymouth and Jamestown all industry was controlled by the commonwealth, and in Massachusetts Bay the stock company had reserved the trade in furs for themselves before leaving England.[129] The trade was frequently

126 U. S. Statutes at Large, III., p. 332. Cf. laws in 1802 and 1822.

127 Wis. Hist. Colls., I., p. 103; Minn. Hist. Colls., V., p. 9. The Warren brothers, who came to Wisconsin in 1818, were descendants of the Pilgrims and related to Joseph Warren who fell at Bunker Hill; they came from Berkshire, Mass., and marrying the half-breed daughters of Michael Cadotte, of La Pointe, succeeded to his trade.

128 See the objections of British traders, Mich. Pioneer Colls., XVI., p. 76ff. The Northwest Company tried to induce the British government to construe the treaty so as to prevent the United States from erecting the forts, urging that a fort at Prairie du Chien would "deprive the Indians of their 'rights and privileges'", guaranteed by the treaty.

129 Mass. Coll. Recs., I., p. 55; III., p. 424.

farmed out, but public "truck houses" were established by the latter colony as early as 1694–5.[130] Franklin, in his public dealings with the Ohio Indians, saw the importance of regulation of the trade, and in 1753 he wrote asking James Bowdoin of Massachusetts to procure him a copy of the truckhouse law of that colony, saying that if it had proved to work well he thought of proposing it for Pennsylvania.[131] The reply of Bowdoin showed that Massachusetts furnished goods to the Indians at wholesale prices and so drove out the French and the private traders. In 1757 Virginia adopted the system for a time,[132] and in 1776 the Continental Congress accepted a plan presented by a committee of which Franklin was a member,[133] whereby £140,000 sterling was expended at the charge of the United Colonies for Indian goods to be sold at moderate prices by factors of the congressional commissioners.[134] The bearing of this act upon the governmental powers of the Congress is worth noting.

In his messages of 1791 and 1792 President Washington urged the need of promoting and regulating commerce with the Indians, and in 1793 he advocated government trading houses. Pickering, of Massachusetts, who was his Secretary of War with the management of Indian affairs, may have strengthened Washington in this design, for he was much interested in Indian improvement, but Washington's own experience had shown him the desirability of some such

130 Acts and Resolves of the Prov. of Mass. Bay, I., p. 172.
131 Bigelow, Franklin's Works, II., pp. 316, 221. A plan for public trading houses came before the Birtish ministry while Franklin was in England, and was commented upon by him for their benefit.
132 Hening, Statutes, VII., p. 116.
133 Journals of Congress, 1775, pp. 162, 168, 247.
134 Ibid., 1776, p. 41.

plan, and he had written to this effect as early as 1783.[135] The objects of Congressional policy in dealing with the Indians were stated by speakers in 1794 as follows:[136] 1. Protection of the frontiersmen from the Indians, by means of the army. 2. Protection of the Indians from the frontiersmen, by laws regulating settlement. 3. Detachment of the Indians from foreign influence, by trading houses where goods could be got cheaply. In 1795 a small appropriation was made for trying the experiment of public trading houses,[137] and in 1796, the same year that the British evacuated the posts, the law which established the system was passed.[138] It was to be temporary, but by re-enactments with alterations it was prolonged until 1822, new posts being added from time to time. In substance the laws provided a certain capital for the Indian trade, the goods to be sold by salaried United States factors, at posts in the Indian country, at such rates as would protect the savage from the extortions of the individual trader, whose actions sometimes provoked hostilities, and would supplant British influence over the Indian. At the same time it was required that the capital stock should not be diminished. In the course of the debate over the law in 1796 considerable *laissez faire* sentiment was called out against the government's becoming a trader, notwithstanding that the purpose of the bill was benevolence and political advantage rather than financial gain.[139] President Jefferson and Secretary Calhoun were friends of the system.[140] It was a failure, however, and under the attacks of

135 Ford's Washington's Writings, X., p. 309.
136 Annals of Cong., IV., p. 1273; cf. *ibid.*, V., p. 231.
137 Amer. State Papers, Ind. Affs., I., p. 583.
138 Annals of Cong., VI., p. 2889.
139 Annals of Congress, V., p. 230 ff., p. 283; Abridgment of Debates, VII., pp. 187–88.
140 Amer. State Papers, Ind. Affs., I., p. 684; II., p. 181.

Senator Benton, the Indian agents and the American Fur Company, it was brought to an end in 1822. The causes of its failure were chiefly these:[141] The private trader went to the hunting grounds of the savages, while the government's posts were fixed. The private traders gave credit to the Indians, which the government did not.[142] The private trader understood the Indians, was related to them by marriage, and was energetic and not over-scrupulous. The government trader was a salaried agent not trained to the work. The private trader sold whiskey and the government did not. The British trader's goods were better than those of the government. The best business principles were not always followed by the superintendent. The system was far from effecting its object, for the Northwestern Indians had been accustomed to receive presents from the British authorities, and had small respect for a government that traded. Upon Wisconsin trade from 1814 to 1822 its influence was slight.

10. Wisconsin Trade in 1820[143]

The goods used in the Indian trade remained much the same from the first, in all sections of the country.[144] They

141 Amer. State Papers, VI., Ind. Affs., II., p. 203; Ind. Treaties, p. 399 *et seq.*; Wis Hist. Colls., VII., p. 269; *Washington Gazette*, 1821, 1822, articles by Ramsay Crooks under signature "Backwoodsman," and speech of Tracy in House of Representatives, February 23, 1821; Benton, Thirty Years View; *id.*, Abr. Deb., VII., p. 1780.

142 To understand the importance of these two points see *post*, pp. 69–73.

143 In an address before the State Historical Society of Wisconsin, on the Character and Influence of the Fur Trade in Wisconsin (Proceedings, 1889, pp. 86–98), I have given details as to Wisconsin settlements, posts, routes of trade, and Indian location and population in 1820.

144 Wis. Hist. Colls., XI., p. 377. Compare the articles used by Radisson, *ante*, p. 33. For La Salle's estimate of amount and kind of goods needed for a post, and the profits thereon, see Penna. Archives, 2d series, VI., pp. 18–19.

were chiefly blankets, coarse cloths, cheap jewelry and trinkets (including strings of wampum), fancy goods (like ribbons, shawls, etc.), kettles, knives, hatchets, guns, powder, tobacco, and intoxicating liquor.[145] These goods, shipped from Mackinaw, at first came by canoes or bateaux,[146] and in the later period by vessel, to a leading post, were there redivided[147] and sent to the various trading posts. The Indians, returning from the hunting grounds to their villages in the spring,[148] set the squaws to making maple sugar,[149] planting corn, watermelons, potatoes, squashes, etc., and a little hunting was carried on. The summer was given over to enjoyment, and in the early period to wars. In the autumn they collected their wild rice, or their corn, and again were ready to start for the hunting grounds, sometimes 300 miles distant. At this juncture the trader, licensed

Brandy was an important item, one beaver selling for a pint. For goods and cost in 1728 see a bill quoted by E. D. Neill, on p. 20, *Mag. West. Hist.*, Nov., 1887. Cf. 4 Mass. Hist. Colls., III, p. 344; Byrd Manuscripts, I., p. 180 ff.; Minn. Hist. Colls., II., p. 46; Senate Doc. No. 90, 22d Cong., 1st Sess., II., p. 42ff.

145 Wis. Fur Trade MSS. Cf. Wis. Hist. Colls., XI., p. 377, and Amer. State Papers, Ind Affs., II., p. 360. The amount of liquor taken to the woods was very great. The French Jesuits had protested against its use in vain (Parkman's Old Régime); the United States prohibited it to no purpose. It was an indispensable part of a trader's outfit. Robert Stuart, agent of the American Fur Company at Mackinaw, once wrote to John Lawe, one of the leading traders at Green Bay, that the 56 bbls. of whiskey which he sends is "enough to last two years, and half drown all the Indians he deals with." See also Wis. Hist. Colls., VII., p. 282; McKenney's Tour to the Lakes, pp. 169, 299–301; McKenney's Memoirs, I., pp. 19–21. An old trader assured me that it was the custom to give five or six gallons of "grog"—one-fourth water—to the hunter when he paid his credits; he thought that only about one-eighth or one-ninth part of the whole sales was in whiskey.

146 A light boat sometimes called a "Mackinaw boat," about 32 feet long, by 6½ to 15 feet wide amidships, and sharp at the ends.

147 See Wis. Hist. Colls., II., p. 108.

148 Minn. Hist. Colls., V., p. 263.

149 See Wis. Hist. Colls., VII., pp. 220, 286; III., p. 235; McKenney's Tour, p. 194; Schoolcraft, Ind. Tribes, II., p. 55. Sometimes a family made 1500 lbs. in a season.

by an Indian agent, arrived upon the scene with his goods, without which no family could subsist, much less collect any quantity of furs.[150] These were bought on credit by the hunter, since he could not go on the hunt for the furs, whereby he paid for his supplies, without having goods and ammunition advanced for the purpose. This system of credits,[151] dating back to the French period, had become systematized so that books were kept, with each Indian's account. The amount to which the hunter was trusted was between $40 and $50, at cost prices, upon which the trader expected a gain of about 100 per cent, so that the average annual value of furs brought in by each hunter to pay his credits should have been between $80 and $100.[152] The amount of the credit varied with the reputation of the

[150] Lewis Cass in Senate Docs., No. 90, 22d Cong., 1st Sess., II., p. 1.

[151] See D'Iberville's plans for relocating Indian tribes by denying them credit at certain posts, Margry, IV., p. 597. The system was used by the Dutch, and the Puritans also; see Weeden, Economic and Social Hist. New Eng., I., p. 98. In 1765, after the French and Indian war, the Chippeways of Chequamegon Bay told Henry, a British trader, that unless he advanced them goods on credit, "their wives and children would perish; for that there were neither ammunition nor clothing left among them." He distributed goods worth 3000 beaver skins. Henry, Travels, pp. 195–96. Cf. Neill, Minnesota, pp. 225–26; N. Y. Col. Docs.. VII., p. 543; Amer. State Papers, Ind. Affs., II., pp. 64, 66, 329, 333–35; North American Review, Jan., 1826, p. 110.

[152] Biddle, an Indian agent, testified in 1822 that while the cost of transporting 100 wt. from New York to Green Bay did not exceed five dollars, which would produce a charge of less than 10 per cent on the original cost, the United States factor charged 50 per cent additional. The United States capital stock was diminished by this trade, however. The private dealers charged much more. Schoolcraft in 1831 estimated that $48.34 in goods and provisions at cost prices was the average annual supply of each hunter, or $6.90 to each soul. The substantial accuracy of this sustained by my data. See Sen. Doc., No. 90, 22d Cong., 1st Sess., II., p. 45; State Papers, No. 7, 18th Cong., 1st Sess., I.; State Papers, No. 54, 18th Cong., 2d Sess., III.; Schoolcraft's Indian Tribes, III., p. 599; Invoice Book, Amer. Fur Co., for 1820, 1821; Wis. Fur Trade MSS. in possession of Wisconsin Historical Society.

hunter for honesty and ability in the chase.[153] Sometimes he was trusted to the amount of three hundred dollars. If one-half the credits were paid in the spring the trader thought that he had done a fair business. The importance of this credit system can hardly be overestimated in considering the influence of the fur trade upon the Indians of Wisconsin, and especially in rendering them dependent upon the earlier settlements of the State.

The system left the Indians at the mercy of the trader when one nation monopolized the field, and it compelled them to espouse the cause of one or other when two nations contended for supremacy over their territory. At the same time it rendered the trade peculiarly adapted to monopoly, for when rivals competed, the trade was demoralized, and the Indian frequently sold to a new trader the furs which he had pledged in advance for the goods of another. When the American Fur Company gained control, they systema-tized matters so that there was no competition between their own agents, and private dealers cut into their trade but little for some years. The unit of trade was at first the beaver skin, or, as the pound of beaver skin came to be called, the "plus."[154] The beaver skin was estimated at a pound and a half, though it sometimes weighed two, in which case an allowance was made. Wampum was used for ornament and in treaty-making, but not as currency. Other furs or Indian

[153] The following is a typical account, taken from the books of Jacques Porlier, of Green Bay, for the year 1823: The Indian Michel bought on credit in the fall: $16 worth of cloth; a trap, $1.00; two and a half yards of cotton, $3.12½; three measures of powder, $1.50; lead, $1.00; a bottle of whiskey, 50 cents, and some other articles, such as a gun worm, making in all a bill of about $25. This he paid in full by bringing in eighty-five muskrats, worth nearly $20; a fox, $1.00, and a mocock of maple sugar, worth $4.00.

[154] A. J. Vieau, who traded in the thirties, gave me this information.

commodities, like maple sugar and wild rice, were bought in terms of beaver. As this animal grew scarcer the unit changed to money. By 1820, when few beaver were marketed in Wisconsin, the term plus stood for one dollar.[155] The muskrat skin was also used as the unit in the later days of the trade.[156] In the southern colonies the pound of deer skin had answered the purpose of a unit.[157]

The goods being trusted to the Indians, the bands separated for the hunting grounds. Among the Chippeways, at least, each family or group had a particular stream or region where it exclusively hunted and trapped.[158] Not only were the hunting grounds thus parcelled out; certain Indians were apportioned to certain traders,[159] so that the industrial activities of Wisconsin at this date were remarkably systematic and uniform. Sometimes the trader followed the Indians

155 For the value of the beaver at different periods and places consult indexes, under "beaver," in N. Y. Col. Docs.; Bancroft, Northwest Coast; Weeden. Economic and Social Hist. New Eng.; and see Morgan, American Beaver, pp. 243–44; Henry Travels, p. 192; 2 Penna. Archives, VI., p. 18; Servent, in Paris Ex. Univ. 1867, Rapports, VI., pp. 117, 123; Proc. Wis. State Hist. Soc., 1889, p. 86.

156 Minn. Hist. Colls. II., p. 46, gives the following table for 1836:

St. Louis Prices		Minn. Price	Nett Gain.
Three pt. blanket	=$3 25	60 rat skins at 20 cents=$12 00	$8 75
1½ yds Stroud	= 2 37	60 rat skins at 20 cents= 12 00	9 63
1 N. W. gun	= 6 50	100 rat skins at 20 cents= 20 00	13 50
1 lb. lead	= 06	2 rat skins at 20 cents= 40	34
1 lb. powder	= 28	10 rat skins at 20 cents= 2 00	1 72
1 tin kettle	= 2 50	60 rat skins at 20 cents= 12 00	9 50
1 knife	= 20	4 rat skins at 20 cents= 80	60
1 lb. tobacco	= 12	8 rat skins at 20 cents= 1 60	1 38
1 looking glass	= 04	4 rat skins at 20 cents= 80	76
1½ yd. scarlet cloth=	3 00	60 rat skins at 20 cents= 12 00	9 00

See also the table of prices in Senate Docs., No. 90, 22d Cong., 1st Sess., II., p. 42 et seq.

157 Douglass, Summary, I., p. 176.

158 Morgan, American Beaver, p. 243.

159 Proc. Wis. Hist. Soc., 1889, pp. 92–98.

to their hunting grounds. From time to time he sent his engagés (hired men), commonly five or six in number, to the various places where the hunting bands were to be found, to collect furs on the debts and to sell goods to those who had not received too large credits, and to the customers of rival traders; this was called "running a deouine."[160] The main wintering post had lesser ones, called "jack-knife posts,"[161] depending on it, where goods were left and the furs gathered in going to and from the main post. By these methods Wisconsin was thoroughly visited by the traders before the "pioneers" arrived.[162]

The kind and amount of furs brought in may be judged by the fact that in 1836, long after the best days of the trade, a single Green Bay firm, Porlier and Grignon, shipped to the American Fur Company about 3600 deer skins, 6000 muskrats, 150 bears, 850 raccoons, besides beavers, otters, fishers, martens, lynxes, foxes, wolves, badgers, skunks, etc., amounting to over $6000.

None of these traders became wealthy; Astor's company absorbed the profits. It required its clerks, or factors, to pay an advance of 81½ per cent on the sterling cost of the blankets, strouds, and other English goods, in order to cover the cost of importation and the expense of transportation from New York to Mackinaw. Articles purchased in New York were charged with 15⅓ per cent advance for transpor-

160 Amer. State Papers, Ind. Affs., II., p. 66.

161 Wis. Hist. Colls., XI., pp. 220, 223.

162 The centers of Wisconsin trade were Green Bay, Prairie du Chien, and La Pointe (on Madelaine island, Chequamegon bay). Lesser points of distribution were Milwaukee and Portage. From these places, by means of the interlacing rivers and the numerous lakes of northern Wisconsin, the whole region was visited by birch canoes or Mackinaw boats.

tation, and each class of purchasers was charged with 33⅓ per cent advance as profit on the aggregate amount.[163]

I estimate, from the data given in the sources cited on page 72, note, that in 1820 between $60,000 and $75,000 worth of goods was brought annually to Wisconsin for the Indian trade. An average outfit for a single clerk at a main post was between $1500 and $2000, and for the dependent posts between $100 and $500. There were probably not over 2000 Indian hunters in the State, and the total Indian population did not much exceed 10,000. Comparing this number with the early estimates for the same tribes, we find that, if the former are trustworthy, by 1820 the Indian tribes that remained in Wisconsin had increased their numbers. But the material is too unsatisfactory to afford any valuable conclusion.

After the sale of their lands and the receipt of money annuities, a change came over the Indian trade. The monopoly held by Astor was broken into, and as competition increased, the sales of whiskey were larger, and for money, which the savage could now pay. When the Indians went to Montreal in the days of the French, they confessed that they could not return with supplies because they wasted their furs upon brandy. The same process now went on at their doors. The traders were not dependent upon the Indian's success in hunting alone; they had his annuities to count on, and so did not exert their previous influence in favor of steady hunting. Moreover, the game was now exploited to a considerable degree, so that Wisconsin was no longer the hunter's paradise that it had been in the days of Dablon and La Salle. The long-settled economic life of the Indian being revolutionized, his business honesty declined,

163 Schoolcraft in Senate Doc. No. 90, 22d Cong., 1st Sess., II., p. 43.

and credits were more frequently lost. The annuities fell into the traders' hands for debts and whiskey. "There is no less than near $420,000 of claims against the Winnebagoes," writes a Green Bay trader at Prairie du Chien, in 1838, "so that if they are all just, the dividend will be but very small for each claimant, as there is only $150,000 to pay that."[164]

By this time the influence of the fur trader had so developed mining in the region of Dubuque, Iowa, Galena, Ill., and southwestern Wisconsin, as to cause an influx of American miners, and here began a new element of progress for Wisconsin. The knowledge of these mines was possessed by the early French explorers, and as the use of firearms spread they were worked more and more by Indians, under the stimulus of the trader. In 1810 Nicholas Boilvin, United States Indian agent at Prairie du Chien, reported that the Indians about the lead mines had mostly abandoned the chase and turned their attention to the manufacture of lead, which they sold to fur traders. In 1825 there were at least 100 white miners in the entire lead region,[165] and by 1829 they numbered in the thousands.

Black Hawk's war came in 1832, and agricultural settlement sought the southwestern part of the State after that campaign. The traders opened country stores, and their establishments were nuclei of settlement.[166] In Wisconsin the Indian trading post was a thing of the past.

The birch canoe and the pack-horse had had their day in western New York and about Montreal. In Wisconsin the age of the voyageur continued nearly through the first third

[164] Lawe to Vieau, in Wis. Fur Trade MSS. See also U. S. Indian Treaties, and Wis. Hist. Colls., V., p. 236.

[165] House Ex. Docs., 19th Cong., 2d Sess., II., No. 7.

[166] For example see the Vieau Narrative in Wis. Hist. Colls., XI., and the Wis. Fur Trade MSS.

75

of this century. It went on in the Far Northwest in substantially the same fashion that has been here described, until quite recently; and in the great North Land tributary to Hudson Bay the *chanson* of the voyageur may still be heard, and the dog-sledge laden with furs jingles across the snowy plains from distant post to distant post.[167]

[167] Butler, Wild North Land; Robinson, Great Fur Land, ch. xv.

VII.

~~~~~~

EFFECTS OF THE TRADING POST

We are now in a position to offer some conclusions as to the influence of the Indian trading post.

I. Upon the savage it had worked a transformation. It found him without iron, hunting merely for food and raiment. It put into his hands iron and guns, and made him a hunter for furs with which to purchase the goods of civilization. Thus it tended to perpetuate the hunter stage; but it must also be noted that for a time it seemed likely to develop a class of merchants who should act as intermediaries solely. The inter-tribal trade between Montreal and the Northwest, and between Albany and the Illinois and Ohio country, appears to have been commerce in the proper sense of the term[1] (*Kauf zum Verkauf*). The trading post left the unarmed tribes at the mercy of those that had bought firearms, and this caused a relocation of the Indian

---

[1] Not withstanding Kulischer's assertion that there is no room for this in primitive society. *Vide* Der Handel auf den primitiven Culturstufen, in *Zeitschrift für Völkerpsychologie und Sprachwissenschaft*, X., No. 4, p. 378. Compare instances of inter-tribal trade given *ante*, pp. 8–9, 29–30.

tribes and an urgent demand for the trader by the remote
and unvisited Indians. It made the Indian dependent on the
white man's supplies. The stage of civilization that could
make a gun and gunpowder was too far above the bow and
arrow stage to be reached by the Indian. Instead of elevating
him the trade exploited him. But at the same time, when
one nation did not monopolize the trade, or when it failed
to regulate its own traders, the trading post gave to the
Indians the means of resistance to agricultural settlement.
The American settlers fought for their farms in Kentucky
and Tennessee at a serious disadvantage, because for over
half a century the Creeks and Cherokees had received arms
and ammunition from the trading posts of the French, the
Spanish and the English. In Wisconsin the settlers came
after the Indian had become thoroughly dependent on the
American traders, and so late that no resistance was made.
The trading post gradually exploited the Indian's hunting
ground. By intermarriages with the French traders the
purity of the stock was destroyed and a mixed race produced.[2] The trader broke down the old totemic divisions,
and appointed chiefs regardless of the Indian social organization, to foster his trade. Indians and traders alike testify
that this destruction of Indian institutions was responsible
for much of the difficulty in treating with them, the tribe
being without a recognized head.[3] The sale of their lands,
made less valuable by the extinction of game, gave them a
new medium of exchange, at the same time that, under the
rivalry of trade, the sale of whiskey increased.

II. Upon the white man the effect of the Indian trading

[2] On the "metis," bois-brulés, or half-breeds, consult Smithsonian Reports,
1879, p. 309, and Robinson, Great Fur Land, ch. iii.
[3] Minn. Hist. Colls., V., p. 135; Biddle to Atkinson, 1819, in Ind. Pam-
phlets, Vol. I., No. 15 (Wis. Hist. Soc. Library).

post was also very considerable. The Indian trade gave both English and French a footing in America. But for the Indian supplies some of the most important settlements would have perished.[4] It invited to exploration: the dream of a water route to India and of mines was always present in the more extensive expeditions, but the effective practical inducement to opening the water systems of the interior, and the thing that made exploration possible, was the fur trade. As has been shown, the Indian eagerly invited the trader. Up to a certain point also the trade fostered the advance of settlements. As long as they were in extension of trade with the Indians they were welcomed. The trading posts were the pioneers of many settlements along the entire colonial frontier. In Wisconsin the sites of our principal cities are the sites of old trading posts, and these earliest fur-trading settlements furnished supplies to the farming, mining and lumbering pioneers. They were centers about which settlement collected after the exploitation of the Indian. Although the efforts of the Indians and of the great trading companies, whose profits depended upon keeping the primitive wilderness, were to obstruct agricultural settlement, as the history of the Northwest and of British America shows, nevertheless reports brought back by the individual trader guided the steps of the agricultural pioneer. The trader was the farmer's pathfinder into some of the richest regions of the continent. Both favorably and unfavorably the influence of the Indian trade on settlement was very great.

The trading post was the strategic point in the rivalry of France and England for the Northwest. The American

[4] Parkman, Pioneers of France, p. 230; Carr, Mounds of the Mississippi, p. 8, n. 8; Smith's Generall Historie, I., pp. 88, 90, 155 (Richmond, 1819).

colonists came to know that the land was worth more than the beaver that built in the streams, but the mother country fought for the Northwest as the field of Indian trade in all the wars from 1689 to 1812. The management of the Indian trade led the government under the lead of Franklin and Washington into trading on its own account, a unique feature of its policy. It was even proposed by the Indian Superintendent at one time that the government should manufacture the goods for this trade. In providing a new field for the individual trader, whom he expected the government trading houses to dispossess, Jefferson proposed the Lewis and Clarke expedition, which crossed the continent by way of the Missouri and the Columbia, as the British trader, Mackenzie, had before crossed it by way of Canadian rivers. The genesis of this expedition illustrates at once the comprehensive western schemes of Jefferson, and the importance of the part played by the fur trade in opening the West. In 1786, while the Annapolis convention was discussing the navigation of the Potomac, Jefferson wrote to Washington from Paris inquiring about the best place for a canal between the Ohio and the Great Lakes.[5] This was in promotion of the project of Ledyard, a Connecticut man, who was then in Paris endeavoring to interest the wealthiest house there in the fur trade of the Far West. Jefferson took so great an interest in the plan that he secured from the house a promise that if they undertook the scheme the depot of supply should be at Alexandria, on the Potomac river, which would be in connection with the Ohio, if the canal schemes of the time were carried out. After the failure of the negotiations of Ledyard, Jefferson proposed to him to cross Russia to Kamschatka, take ship to Nootka Sound, and

5 Jefferson, Works, II., pp. 60, 250, 370.

thence return to the United States by way of the Missouri.[6] Ledyard was detained in Russia by the authorities in spite of Jefferson's good offices, and the scheme fell through. But Jefferson himself asserts that this suggested the idea of the Lewis and Clarke expedition, which he proposed to Congress as a means of fostering our Indian trade.[7] Bearing in mind his instructions to this party, that they should see whether the Oregon furs might not be shipped down the Missouri instead of passing around Cape Horn, and the relation of his early canal schemes to this design, we see that he had conceived the project of a transcontinental fur trade which should center in Virginia. Astor's subsequent attempt to push through a similar plan resulted in the foundation of his short-lived post of Astoria at the mouth of the Columbia. This occupation greatly aided our claim to the Oregon country as against the British traders, who had reached the region by way of the northern arm of the Columbia.

In Wisconsin, at least, the traders' posts, placed at the carrying places around falls and rapids, pointed out the water powers of the State. The portages between rivers became canals, or called out canal schemes that influenced the early development of the State. When Washington, at the close of his military service, inspected the Mohawk valley and the portages between the headwaters of the Potomac and the Ohio, as the channels "of conveyance of the extensive and valuable trade of a rising empire,"[8] he stood between two eras—the era with which he was personally

[6] Allen's Lewis and Clarke Expedition, p. ix (edition of 1814. The introduction is by Jefferson).

[7] Jefferson's messages of January 18, 1803, and February 19, 1806. See Amer. State Papers, Ind. Affs., I., p. 684.

[8] See Adams, Maryland's Influence upon Land Cessions to U. S., J. H. U. Studies, 3d Series, No. I., pp. 80–82.

familiar, when these routes had been followed by the trader with the savage tribes,[9] and the era which he foresaw, when American settlement passed along the same ways to the fertile West and called into being the great trunk-lines of the present day.[10] The trails became the early roads. An old Indian trader relates that "the path between Green Bay and Milwaukee was originally an Indian trail, and very crooked, but the whites would straighten it by cutting across lots each winter with their jumpers, wearing bare streaks through the thin covering, to be followed in the summer by foot and horseback travel along the shortened path."[11] The process was typical of a greater one. Along the lines that nature had drawn the Indians traded and warred; along their trails and in their birch canoes the trader passed, bringing a new and a transforming life. These slender lines of eastern influence stretched throughout all our vast and intricate water-system, even to the Gulf of Mexico, the Pacific, and the Arctic seas, and these lines were in turn followed by agricultural and by manufacturing civilization.

In a speech upon the Pacific Railway delivered in the United States Senate in 1850, Senator Benton used these words: "There is an idea become current of late . . . that none but a man of science, bred in a school, can lay off a road. That is a mistake. There is a class of topographical

9 *Ibid. Vide ante*, p. 46.

10 Narr. and Crit. Hist. Amer., VIII., p. 10. Compare Adams, as above. At Jefferson's desire, in January and February of 1788, Washington wrote various letters inquiring as to the feasibility of a canal between Lake Erie and the Ohio, "whereby the fur and peltry of the upper country can be transported"; saying: "Could a channel once be opened to convey the fur and peltry from the Lakes into the eastern country, its advantages would be so obvious as to induce an opinion that it would in a short time become the channel of conveyance for much the greater part of the commodities brought from thence." Sparks, Washington's Works, IX., pp. 303, 327.

11 Wis. Hist. Colls., XI., p. 230.

engineers older than the schools, and more unerring than the mathematics. They are the wild animals—buffalo, elk, deer, antelope, bears, which traverse the forest, not by compass, but by an instinct which leads them always the right way—to the lowest passes in the mountains, the shallowest fords in the rivers, the richest pastures in the forest, the best salt springs, and the shortest practicable routes between remote points. They travel thousands of miles, have their annual migrations backwards and forwards, and never miss the best and shortest route. These are the first engineers to lay out a road in a new country; the Indians follow them, and hence a buffalo-road becomes a war-path. The first white hunters follow the same trails in pursuing their game; and after that the buffalo-road becomes the wagon-road of the white man, and finally the macadamized or railroad of the scientific man. It all resolves itself into the same thing—into the same buffalo-road; and thence the buffalo becomes the first and safest engineer. Thus it has been here in the countries which we inhabit and the history of which is so familiar. The present national road from Cumberland over the Alleghanies was the military road of General Braddock; which had been the buffalo-path of the wild animals. So of the two roads from western Virginia to Kentucky—one through the gap in the Cumberland mountains, the other down the valley of the Kenhawa. They were both the war-path of the Indians and the travelling route of the buffalo, and their first white acquaintances the early hunters. Buffaloes made them in going from the salt springs on the Holston to the rich pastures and salt springs of Kentucky; Indians followed them first, white hunters afterwards—and that is the way Kentucky was discovered. In more than a hundred years no nearer or better routes have been found; and science now makes her improved roads exactly where the buffalo's foot first marked the way and the hunter's foot afterwards followed him. So all over Kentucky and the West; and so in the Rocky Mountains. The famous South Pass was no scientific discovery. Some people think Fremont discovered it. It had been discovered forty years before—long before he was born. He only described it and confirmed what the hunters and traders had reported and what they showed him. It was discovered, or rather first seen by white people, in 1808, two years after the return of Lewis and Clark, and by the first company of hunters and traders that went out after their report laid open the prospect of the fur trade in the Rocky Mountains.

"An enterprising Spaniard of St. Louis, Manuel Lisa, sent out the party; an acquaintance and old friend of the Senator from Wisconsin who sits on my left [General Henry Dodge] led the party—his name Andrew Henry. He was the first man that saw that pass; and he found it in the prosecution of his business, that of a hunter and trader, and by following the game and the road which they had made. And that is the way all passes are found. But these traders do not write books and make maps, but they enable other people to do it."[12]

Benton errs in thinking that the hunter was the pioneer in Kentucky. As I have shown, the trader opened the way. But Benton is at least valid authority upon the Great West, and his fundamental thesis has much truth in it. A continuously higher life flowed into the old channels, knitting the

12 Cong. Rec., XXIII., p. 57. I found this interesting confirmation of my views after this paper was written. Compare *Harper's Magazine*, Sept. 1890, p. 565.

United States together into a complex organism. It is a
process not limited to America. In every country the exploitation of the wild beasts,[13] and of the raw products generally,
causes the entry of the disintegrating and transforming influences of a higher civilization. "The history of commerce
is the history of the intercommunication of peoples."

[13] The traffic in furs in the Middle Ages was enormous, says Friedländer,
Sittengeschichte, III., p. 62. Numerous cities in England and on the Continent, whose names are derived from the word "beaver" and whose seals
bear the beaver, testify to the former importance in Europe of this animal;
see Canadian Journal, 1859, p. 359. See Du Chaillu, Viking Age, pp. 209–10;
Marco Polo, bk. iv., ch. xxi. Wattenbach, in Historische Zeitschrift, IX.,
p. 391, shows that German traders were known in the lands about the Baltic
at least as early as the knights.

INDEX

Accault (trader): 34
Adams, Herbert Baxter: xiii, xvi
Africa: 4, 6
Agriculture: 13, 24ff.
Alabama: 17
Albany: 14, 15, 77: *see also* Orange
Alexandria, Va.: 80
Algonquin Indians: 8, 15
Allegheny Mountains: 16, 83
Allouez, Claude Jean (Jesuit): 25–26, 32
American Fur Company: 59n., 64–65, 68, 69n., 71, 73
American Historical Association, Executive Council of: vii
American Revolution: 44, 50
Annapolis Convention of 1786: 80
Arctic Sea: 22, 82
Astor, John Jacob: 19, 29, 63, 65, 73–74, 81
Astoria: 64, 81
Augusta, Ga.: 18

Bacon's Rebellion: 16
Bancroft, George: 33

Beaujeau (French commander): 46
Becker, Carl: xii
Benton, Thomas Hart: 19, 20, 68, 82–84
Berkshire, Mass.: 65n.
Biddle (Indian agent): 70n.
Billington, Ray Allen: xi
Black Hawk War: 29, 75
Blue Ridge Mountains: 18
Boilvin, Nicholas: 75
Bois Brulé River: 23
Bonaparte, Napoleon: 56
Boone, Daniel: 18
Bowdoin, James: 66
Braddock, Edward: 47, 83
Bradford, William: 12
Breton sailors: 21
Bunker Hill, Battle of: 65n.

Cabot, John: 21
Cadotte, Michael: 65n.
Calhoun, John C.: 67
California: 19
Calumet: 7
Canada: 20n., 22, 24ff.

87

The paper on which this book is printed bears the water-mark of the University of Oklahoma Press and has an effective life of at least three hundred years.